The Evergreen Spellbook

The Evergreen Spellbook

Matthew Petchinsky

The Evergreen Spellbook
By: Matthew Petchinsky

Introduction to *The Evergreen Spellbook*
Welcome to the Evergreen Spellbook

Welcome, seekers of the ancient and mystical arts, to *The Evergreen Spellbook*. This collection was created to guide both novice and experienced practitioners through a journey of nature-inspired spells that resonate with the power of the natural world. Here, you will discover rituals and enchantments woven from the wisdom of the earth, elements, and timeless traditions. Each chapter unfolds a spell crafted to offer practical benefits and enrich your life, drawing from the heart of the evergreen forest, where magic is as ageless as the trees.

Within these pages, you will not only learn spells but also the stories and symbolism behind them, empowering you to tap into the boundless energy of the natural world. This book is designed to be more than just a manual—it's a guide to connecting with the rhythm of nature and awakening the enchantment within you.

Harnessing Nature's Power

Nature has been revered for millennia as a source of power, wisdom, and harmony. Our ancestors understood that the wind carried whispers of change, the trees stood as guardians, and rivers mirrored the continuous flow of life. The world around us is alive with energy, waiting for those attuned to its presence to channel and shape it for their needs.

This spellbook emphasizes the importance of working harmoniously with natural energies, utilizing the sun, moon, earth, and all elements in between. By drawing from these ancient sources, the spells here are more than incantations; they are extensions of the natural world's heartbeat. This practice is not about controlling nature but about partnering with it, fostering a relationship built on respect, gratitude, and understanding.

Using This Spellbook for Daily Enchantment

The Evergreen Spellbook is structured for ease of use, allowing you to choose spells based on your immediate needs or long-term goals. Whether you seek to manifest abundance, protect your home, promote inner peace, or create meaningful connections, this book has a spell that aligns with your intentions. Each spell includes clear, step-by-step instructions and an explanation of its purpose, so you can confidently bring enchantment into your everyday life.

To use this spellbook effectively:

- **Set Your Intention:** Begin each spell with a clear mind and focus on your desired outcome.
- **Choose the Right Timing:** Some spells are more potent during specific times, such as full moons or at sunrise. These details are noted to help you achieve the best results.
- **Prepare with Care:** Gather the required materials and create a peaceful space where you can perform the spell without interruptions.

Integrate these practices into your daily life to keep your connection with nature strong and vibrant.

Safety Tips and Precautions for Spellcasting

While spellcasting can be a powerful and transformative experience, it's essential to approach it with mindfulness and caution. Below are some key safety tips to ensure your practice is both effective and safe:

1. **Respect the Elements:** Working with fire, herbs, or sharp tools should always be done with care. Keep water or a fire extinguisher nearby when working with flames, and handle sharp objects with steady hands.
2. **Understand Herbal Properties:** Some plants and herbs can be toxic or may cause allergic reactions. Familiarize yourself with the properties of each herb before use.
3. **Create a Safe Space:** Perform your rituals in a space that is free from distractions and potential hazards. Ensure you're in a well-ventilated area when burning incense or herbs.
4. **Ground and Center:** Before starting any spell, take a moment to ground yourself. This practice not only protects your energy but also stabilizes your focus.
5. **Respect Boundaries:** Only perform spells that align with your moral compass and avoid influencing others without their consent.

Approaching each spell with awareness and precaution will help you create an environment where magic can flourish safely and effectively.

Materials and Tools You'll Need

Every spell in *The Evergreen Spellbook* uses materials sourced from nature or items that are easily accessible. To make your journey smooth and inspiring, here is a list of common materials and tools you'll encounter in the book:

- **Herbs and Plants:** Fresh or dried (e.g., sage, lavender, rosemary)
- **Crystals and Stones:** Amethyst, quartz, citrine, and other stones that align with specific intentions
- **Natural Elements:** Water, sand, soil, and branches from certain trees
- **Incense and Essential Oils:** To add aromatic and symbolic significance to your spells
- **Candles:** White, green, blue, and other colored candles depending on the spell's purpose
- **Ritual Tools:** Chalice, athame, wand, and a small cauldron for burning or mixing ingredients
- **Paper and Pen:** For recording your intentions and results
- **Natural Fibers:** Such as twine or cloth for binding and knot magic

These tools, combined with the spells in this book, will help you create rituals that are powerful, meaningful, and seamlessly integrated into your life. Remember, the most important tool is your intent—focus it well, and nature will respond in kind.

Welcome to your enchanted journey into *The Evergreen Spellbook*. Let the power of nature and your own spirit guide you through each spell, as you bring harmony and magic into your world.

Chapter 1: Spell of Sunrise Energy
Harnessing the first light of dawn for vitality and focus

Introduction to the Spell

The early morning sun is a powerful source of revitalizing energy. It carries the promise of a new beginning, infuses life with vigor, and offers a profound moment of connection to the natural world. The *Spell of Sunrise Energy* is designed to harness this vibrant energy to awaken your inner strength and sharpen your focus for the day ahead. This spell is especially effective when practiced regularly, as it fosters a deep and lasting bond with the sun's life-giving rays.

Significance of Dawn Energy

Dawn represents a threshold—a bridge between the quiet of the night and the awakening of day. The energy at sunrise is considered pure and untarnished, making it ideal for spells that invoke vitality, renewal, and clarity. When you perform this ritual, you align your body and spirit with the sun's ascension, allowing its rays to infuse you with strength and focus that can last throughout the day.

Ideal Timing and Preparations

- **Best Time for the Ritual:** Perform this spell at dawn, when the first rays of sunlight break over the horizon. Check local sunrise times to ensure you're ready when the moment arrives.
- **Location:** Ideally, perform this ritual outdoors in a space where you have an unobstructed view of the sunrise. If outdoor rituals aren't possible, a window that faces the east will suffice.
- **Clothing:** Wear comfortable, loose clothing in light colors, preferably white or yellow, to symbolize the sun's radiance.
- **Mindset:** Approach the ritual with a clear mind and a heart open to receiving the sun's gifts.

Materials Needed

- A small bowl of fresh water
- A yellow or orange candle (to represent the sun)
- A quartz crystal (for amplifying energy)
- A piece of paper and a pen
- A cup of herbal tea (optional, for grounding after the ritual)

The Ritual: Step-by-Step Guide

1. **Set Up Your Space** Begin by finding a quiet, serene space with a view of the eastern horizon. Place the bowl of water in front of you and position the candle beside it. Hold the quartz crystal in your hands for a moment, feeling its cool, smooth surface, and focus on your intention of gaining vitality and focus.
2. **Ground and Center** Sit comfortably with your feet planted firmly on the ground. Close your eyes, take three deep breaths, and visualize roots extending from the soles of your feet into the earth. Feel your connection to the ground as a stabilizing force.
3. **Light the Candle** Light the yellow or orange candle and say: *"I call upon the morning sun,*
Source of life and light,
Fill me with your strength and clarity,
Let your energy be my might."
4. **Gaze at the Rising Sun** Open your eyes and direct your gaze towards the horizon. As the sun begins to rise, observe its golden rays spreading across the sky. Visualize this light enveloping your body in a warm, energizing glow. Feel the warmth soaking into your skin, filling your entire being with vitality and renewed energy.ASX
5. **Invoke the Energy** Dip your fingers into the bowl of water and touch it to your forehead, heart, and hands, saying: *"By the touch*

*of water and the light of dawn,
I welcome vitality; I embrace focus.
With each breath, I am empowered,
With each heartbeat, I am attuned."*

6. **Amplify with the Crystal** Hold the quartz crystal in your dominant hand and raise it toward the rising sun. Imagine the crystal absorbing the morning's light and channeling that energy into your body. Visualize it radiating warmth through your palm, up your arm, and into your core.
7. **Seal Your Intention** On the piece of paper, write a short affirmation such as: *"I am energized and focused throughout my day."* Place the paper near the candle and say: *"This day is blessed, this day is bright.
I carry the sun's power into my life."*
8. **Conclude and Ground Yourself** Blow out the candle and close the ritual by sipping the herbal tea, allowing its warmth to ground you. If you're outdoors, touch the ground briefly to reinforce your connection with the earth.

After the Ritual: Tips for Maximizing Benefits

- **Daily Affirmation:** Throughout the day, repeat the affirmation you wrote to keep the energy of the sunrise within you.
- **Crystal Use:** Keep the quartz crystal with you to serve as a reminder of the morning's spell and to sustain the vitality you summoned.
- **Reflection:** Spend a few minutes journaling after the ritual. Write about how the morning energy made you feel and any intentions you wish to carry forward.

Practical Applications of the Spell

The *Spell of Sunrise Energy* is especially beneficial on days when you need an extra boost, whether for work, creative projects, or any demanding activity. Regular practice helps build a routine of mindfulness and focus, grounding your day in purposeful energy. As you continue this ritual, you may find that your mornings become moments of sacred connection, fueling not just your body but your spirit.

Embrace the spell's power and let the dawn renew your essence daily. Welcome the sunrise, and let its light illuminate the path ahead with unwavering strength and clarity.

Chapter 2: Whispering Wind Communication Spell
A practical spell for clear communication in important conversations

Introduction to the Spell

Effective communication is at the heart of all relationships, whether they be personal, professional, or spiritual. Yet, even with the best intentions, misunderstandings can arise, leading to frustration and discord. The *Whispering Wind Communication Spell* is designed to enhance clarity in speech and understanding during important conversations. This ritual calls upon the air element—traditionally associated with intellect, communication, and connection—to infuse your interactions with truth, ease, and mutual comprehension.

The Power of the Air Element

The wind carries messages and whispers secrets between the leaves. In many ancient traditions, air is seen as the bridge between thoughts and spoken words. Harnessing the energy of this element helps align your intentions with your voice, ensuring that your message is heard and understood. This spell channels the movement and freedom of the wind to remove barriers that hinder communication and foster an environment where dialogue can flourish.

Ideal Timing and Preparations

- **Best Time for the Ritual:** This spell works best when performed on a breezy day or when there is a gentle wind, symbolizing the movement of air. If this is not possible, a quiet room with an open window or a fan will suffice.
- **Moon Phase:** Performing this spell during a waxing or full moon can enhance the energy and intention behind it, though it is effective at any time.

- **Location:** Choose a place where you can feel or hear the wind, such as a garden, balcony, or park.
- **Mindset:** Approach this spell with an open heart and a clear sense of the communication issue you wish to address.

Materials Needed

- A feather (symbolizing air and lightness)
- A small, hand-held bell or wind chime
- A slip of paper and a pen
- Lavender essential oil or a small bundle of dried lavender
- A blue or white candle (to represent the air element)

The Ritual: Step-by-Step Guide

1. **Create Your Sacred Space** Find a quiet spot where you can comfortably perform the ritual. Set up your candle and other materials, ensuring that you feel at ease in your surroundings. If possible, sit where you can feel the wind or a breeze brushing against your skin.
2. **Ground Yourself** Close your eyes and take deep, calming breaths. Visualize roots growing from the base of your spine into the ground, anchoring you firmly. Feel the stability of the earth beneath you and the lightness of the air around you.
3. **Anoint the Candle** Apply a few drops of lavender essential oil to the blue or white candle, infusing it with the intention of peaceful and clear communication. Light the candle and say: *"By this flame, I call upon the clarity of the wind,*
To carry my words and intentions true."
4. **Write Your Intention** On the slip of paper, write down a concise statement that embodies your intention for the conversation. For example, *"May my words be clear, and may understanding flow between us."*

5. **Invoke the Air Element** Hold the feather in one hand and gently wave it, mimicking the flow of the wind. As you do, ring the bell or shake the wind chime lightly to invite the air element to your space. Say: *"Winds of change, winds so wise,*
Bring clarity; lift the veil from eyes.
Carry my voice, calm and clear,
So hearts will listen, so minds will hear."
6. **Focus on the Wind** Spend a moment with your eyes closed, feeling the air around you. Visualize the wind picking up your words, carrying them gently but firmly to their destination. Imagine it clearing any blockages or misunderstandings between you and the person you need to communicate with.
7. **Seal the Intention** Hold the slip of paper close to your mouth and whisper your intention into it. Then, place the paper under the candle and say: *"This message now rides the wind's breath,*
To bring understanding, free from distress."
8. **Conclude and Ground** Extinguish the candle and say a final word of gratitude: *"Thank you, winds, for your guidance and grace.*
Your energy, now in its rightful place."

Place the feather and paper in a safe spot, such as on your altar or in a special box, as a reminder of your intention.

Post-Ritual Tips for Success

- **Carry the Feather:** Keep the feather with you when you engage in the important conversation as a tangible symbol of the air element's assistance.
- **Mindful Listening:** Remember that communication is a two-way street. Use this spell to remain as open and attentive to others as you wish them to be to you.
- **Repeat if Needed:** If the conversation is complex or ongoing, you can repeat the spell as needed to maintain a clear channel of communication.

Enhancements for More Potency

- **Add Aromatherapy:** Burn lavender or rosemary incense during the ritual to further enhance mental clarity and promote peaceful exchanges.
- **Crystals for Support:** If desired, hold a piece of aquamarine or blue lace agate during the spell, as these stones are known for aiding communication and calming emotions.
- **Affirmations:** In the days leading up to the conversation, repeat affirmations such as *"My words flow with ease, and understanding surrounds me."*

Practical Applications of the Spell

This spell is especially helpful before important discussions, such as job interviews, negotiations, or heartfelt conversations with loved ones. It is also useful for any situation where clear, assertive communication is vital, like public speaking or mediating conflicts.

By performing the *Whispering Wind Communication Spell*, you call upon the natural element of air to be your ally in creating conversations that are grounded in honesty, understanding, and respect. Let the wind carry your words and intentions, ensuring they are met with open ears and receptive minds.

Chapter 3: Hearth Warming Home Blessing

A spell to invite warmth, protection, and love into your home

Introduction to the Spell

Home is more than just a physical space; it is a sanctuary where we seek comfort, love, and safety. The *Hearth Warming Home Blessing* spell is designed to infuse your living space with warmth, protection, and an energy that nurtures all who enter. Drawing on the elemental power of fire—traditionally associated with the hearth—this spell channels its qualities to create an atmosphere of well-being and security.

This ritual can be performed whenever you move into a new home, during significant life transitions, or simply when your space needs a revitalizing boost. By inviting the energies of love and protection into your dwelling, you create an environment where harmony and positive energy can flourish.

The Significance of the Hearth

Historically, the hearth was the center of the home, symbolizing not only warmth and nourishment but also community and protection. It was the place where stories were shared, meals were prepared, and families gathered. The energy of the hearth is powerful, embodying the essence of protection and connection. This spell draws on that legacy, modernized for use in any space, whether you have a traditional hearth or not.

Ideal Timing and Preparations

- **Best Time for the Ritual:** Perform this spell on a Sunday (the day of the Sun) or on a day when you want to infuse your space with warm, protective energy. It is most effective in the late afternoon or early evening.
- **Moon Phase:** The waxing or full moon amplifies the energy of growth and positive change, but this spell can be done at any time as needed.

- **Location:** This ritual should be conducted in a central part of your home, preferably near the living room or an area where family and friends gather frequently.
- **Mindset:** Approach the ritual with a heart full of love and gratitude, visualizing your home as a welcoming and protected space.

Materials Needed

- A small bowl of sea salt (for purification)
- A red or orange candle (to represent the hearth)
- Dried herbs such as rosemary, sage, or bay leaves (for protection and love)
- A fire-safe bowl or cauldron
- A piece of paper and a pen
- A bundle of cinnamon sticks (symbolizing warmth and prosperity)
- A small dish of honey or a sweet treat (as an offering to the protective energies)

The Ritual: Step-by-Step Guide

1. **Create Your Sacred Space** Begin by tidying up the area where you will perform the spell. Cleanliness helps clear stagnant energy, making it easier to invite new, positive vibrations. Place the candle in the center of the room and arrange the other materials around it.
2. **Ground and Center** Stand or sit comfortably with your feet planted firmly on the ground. Close your eyes, take a deep breath, and visualize roots extending from your body into the earth, grounding you. As you breathe in, feel warmth radiating up through these roots and filling your body.
3. **Light the Candle** Light the red or orange candle and say: *"Sacred flame, source of warmth and light,*

*Fill this home with love so bright.
Guard it well, keep it strong,
May its walls sing a protective song."*

4. **Purify the Space** Sprinkle a small amount of sea salt in the four corners of the room to purify and protect the space. As you do, visualize a protective barrier forming around your home, keeping negativity at bay.
5. **Write Your Intention** On the piece of paper, write down a heartfelt intention for your home. For example: *"May this home be filled with warmth, love, and protection, bringing comfort and joy to all who enter."* Hold the paper close to your heart and take a moment to feel the sincerity of your intention.
6. **Burn the Herbs** Place the dried rosemary, sage, or bay leaves in the fire-safe bowl or cauldron. Light them carefully and let the smoke waft through the room. As the smoke rises, say: *"By the smoke of sacred herbs,
I call forth blessings, love, and verve.
May this home be a fortress true,
Sheltered and blessed in all we do."*
7. **Symbolic Offering** Place the bundle of cinnamon sticks and the dish of honey near the candle as a symbolic offering. The cinnamon brings warmth and prosperity, while the honey symbolizes sweetness and harmony in the household.
8. **Seal the Intention** Hold the paper with your written intention over the candle (without letting it catch fire) and say: *"With this flame, I seal my prayer,
A home of warmth beyond compare.
Protection, love, within these walls,
A sacred space where joy befalls."*

Place the paper under the candle or in a safe, special place within your home.

1. **Close the Ritual** Extinguish the candle with gratitude, saying:
   "Thank you, flame, for your radiant gift,
   May your warmth in this home forever lift."

Allow the smoke from the herbs to settle, and take a moment to feel the energy in the room. Visualize the home glowing with a soft, protective light that expands to every corner and crevice.

Post-Ritual Maintenance

- **Reinforce with Daily Practices:** Maintain the energy of the blessing by lighting the candle for a few minutes each evening or during times of family gatherings.
- **Add Fresh Energy:** Place cinnamon sticks in your kitchen or common areas to continuously invite warmth and prosperity.
- **Weekly Cleansing:** Burn a small amount of sage or use a sound-clearing method (such as ringing a bell) once a week to refresh the protective energy.

Enhancements for More Potency

- **Aromatherapy Addition:** Diffuse essential oils such as orange, cinnamon, or clove to enhance the feeling of warmth and protection.
- **Crystals for Support:** Place protective crystals like black tourmaline or obsidian near entry points of your home to amplify the spell's effects.
- **Family Involvement:** For a deeper impact, involve family members by asking them to contribute their own intentions for the home and share in the ritual.

Practical Applications of the Spell

The *Hearth Warming Home Blessing* is particularly useful during life changes such as moving to a new place, preparing for a holiday gathering, or after difficult times that may have disrupted the harmony of your space. This spell not only protects your home but also fills it with the nurturing, loving energy that creates a true sanctuary.

Perform this spell and watch as your home becomes a haven where love thrives, warmth permeates, and all who enter feel its welcoming embrace.

Chapter 4: The Hidden Pathway Finder

A nature-based spell to reveal new opportunities or hidden solutions

Introduction to the Spell

Life often presents us with challenges that seem insurmountable or complex situations where the right course of action is unclear. The *Hidden Pathway Finder* spell is designed to illuminate these unseen possibilities and reveal solutions that may not be immediately apparent. This nature-based spell taps into the wisdom of the earth, the subtle whispers of the wind, and the guidance of ancient energies to help you see beyond the obvious and discover the path that lies hidden before you.

This spell is especially beneficial when you are at a crossroads or facing decisions that require creative thinking or insight. It helps you draw on the intuitive power of nature to guide you toward fresh perspectives and unexplored opportunities.

The Power of Nature's Wisdom

Nature is a master of adaptation and resourcefulness. Trees find sunlight even in dense forests, water carves paths through mountains, and roots break through stone to nourish the plant above. This innate ability to find a way where there seems to be none is what this spell harnesses. By aligning yourself with these natural forces, you can channel the earth's ingenuity to uncover hidden paths in your own life.

Ideal Timing and Preparations

- **Best Time for the Ritual:** This spell works best when performed at dawn or dusk, times of transition that symbolize new beginnings and the unveiling of possibilities.

- **Moon Phase:** The waxing moon, full moon, or new moon are optimal phases for this spell, as they signify growth, illumination, and new opportunities.
- **Location:** An outdoor space surrounded by nature, such as a park, garden, or forest, is ideal. If an outdoor setting is not possible, create an indoor space with natural elements such as plants, stones, and fresh air by an open window.
- **Mindset:** Approach the ritual with an open mind, ready to receive guidance and clarity.

Materials Needed

- A smooth stone or pebble (to represent grounding and guidance)
- A small, green candle (to symbolize growth and discovery)
- Dried leaves or a small bundle of herbs like thyme or basil (for clarity and insight)
- A piece of paper and a pen
- A bowl of water
- A small wooden stick or twig (to trace symbols)
- A journal (optional, for reflections)

The Ritual: Step-by-Step Guide

1. **Create Your Sacred Space** Begin by setting up your ritual space in a peaceful area where you feel connected to nature. Place the green candle in the center and arrange the stone, herbs, bowl of water, and wooden stick around it.
2. **Ground and Center** Stand or sit comfortably, feet touching the earth or floor. Close your eyes and take a few deep, slow breaths. Visualize roots growing from the base of your spine into the ground, anchoring you firmly to the earth. Feel the energy of the ground below you, stable and wise, supporting you.

3. **Light the Candle** Light the green candle and say: *"Flame of growth, light my way,*
   Guide my path, both night and day.
   Reveal what's hidden, make clear and true,
   The path I seek, the course I pursue."
4. **Trace the Symbol of Insight** Using the wooden stick, trace an eye or a spiral symbol (representing discovery and intuition) in the air above the candle. Imagine the symbol glowing with energy and clarity.
5. **Infuse the Stone with Intention** Hold the smooth stone in your dominant hand and close your eyes. Whisper your specific need or question into the stone. For example, you might say, *"Show me the way to find a solution for [state your situation]."* Visualize the stone absorbing your words and intention, becoming a vessel of insight and guidance.
6. **Offer the Leaves to the Wind** Take the dried leaves or herbs in your hands, hold them close to your heart, and say: *"Leaves of wisdom, hear my plea,*
   Carry my voice, let truth come to me.
   Lift the veil, open my sight,
   Reveal the path that's hidden from light."

Let the leaves or herbs scatter gently in the breeze, or if indoors, place them in the bowl of water as an offering to nature's energy.

1. **Reflection with the Water** Dip your fingers into the bowl of water and touch your forehead, whispering: *"With clarity's touch, let my mind be clear,*
   Show me the hidden, what I should hold dear."

As you look into the water, take a moment to meditate on the surface. If any thoughts, images, or sensations arise, note them mentally or in your journal later. These might be the first clues to your hidden pathway.

1. **Seal the Intention** Place the stone beside the candle and say:
   "Stone of earth, guide my way,
   With strength and vision day by day.
   Path unseen, now appear,
   With wisdom and courage, draw me near."
2. **Close the Ritual** Extinguish the candle and offer thanks to the guiding forces of nature: *"Thank you, earth, and thank you, air,*
   For showing me paths with wisdom rare.
   Your energy now is mine to hold,
   As new paths and stories unfold."

Post-Ritual Practices

- **Keep the Stone Close:** Carry the infused stone with you or place it on your nightstand to keep the energy of the spell active.
- **Reflect and Journal:** Over the next few days, keep an eye out for signs, sudden inspirations, or moments of clarity that reveal new opportunities. Write down any significant dreams or observations.
- **Repeat as Needed:** This spell can be repeated whenever you seek guidance on new opportunities or solutions.

Enhancements for More Potency

- **Add Essential Oils:** Dab a few drops of essential oil such as eucalyptus or peppermint on your stone before infusing it with intention to boost mental clarity.
- **Crystals for Amplification:** Include a clear quartz or amethyst crystal in the ritual to enhance intuitive abilities and spiritual insight.

- **Affirmations for Clarity:** In the days following the spell, repeat affirmations such as *"I am open to new paths and creative solutions."*

Practical Applications of the Spell

The *Hidden Pathway Finder* spell is especially useful when facing complex life decisions, problem-solving in work or personal life, or during periods of uncertainty when a fresh perspective is needed. It helps channel nature's boundless resourcefulness and quiet guidance to illuminate options you may not have seen before.

Perform this spell with an open heart and trust that nature will reveal what is meant to be seen. New paths, opportunities, and solutions will begin to emerge, leading you forward with newfound confidence and clarity.

Chapter 5: Moonlit Reflection Spell
A ritual for clarity and introspection during full moon nights

Introduction to the Spell

The full moon has long been regarded as a powerful symbol of illumination, mystery, and transformation. Its silvery light casts away shadows and reveals what lies beneath the surface, making it the perfect companion for introspection and seeking clarity. The *Moonlit Reflection Spell* harnesses the energy of the full moon to enhance self-awareness, aid in deep reflection, and guide you toward clarity in your thoughts and emotions. This ritual is ideal for those who seek insight into personal challenges, life paths, or emotional states.

The spell uses the moon's natural energy to bring hidden truths to light, offering a clear view of your inner world. By performing this ritual, you align yourself with the moon's cycles, deepening your connection to its rhythm and using its gentle, revealing glow to gain a better understanding of yourself.

The Power of the Full Moon

In many spiritual traditions, the full moon represents the peak of energy, a time when the veil between the conscious and subconscious is thin, making it an ideal moment for introspection and clarity. The moon's reflective light not only illuminates the physical world but also acts as a mirror for the soul, allowing hidden thoughts, suppressed emotions, and buried truths to surface. This spell leverages that illuminating energy to guide you toward understanding and personal insight.

Ideal Timing and Preparations

- **Best Time for the Ritual:** This spell should be performed on a full moon night when the moon is high and bright in the sky.

The energy is strongest during this phase and can be felt one day before and one day after the full moon.
- **Location:** An outdoor space where you can sit under the moonlight is ideal. If performing indoors, set up near a window with an unobstructed view of the moon.
- **Mindset:** Approach this ritual with a sense of openness and a willingness to explore your inner self.

Materials Needed

- A silver or white candle (to symbolize the moon's light)
- A small mirror (to reflect the moon's energy)
- A bowl of spring or purified water
- Moonstone or selenite crystal (for enhancing intuition)
- A piece of paper and a pen
- Lavender or jasmine essential oil (to promote relaxation)
- A soft cloth or shawl (optional, for comfort)

The Ritual: Step-by-Step Guide

1. **Prepare Your Space** Choose a serene spot where the moonlight can touch your space. Arrange the candle, mirror, bowl of water, and crystal in a circle around you. Lightly anoint the candle with lavender or jasmine oil to create a calming atmosphere. Place the mirror so that it can catch and reflect the moonlight.
2. **Ground and Center** Sit comfortably with your feet touching the ground or floor. Close your eyes and take a few deep, slow breaths. Imagine roots growing from your body, anchoring you firmly to the earth. With each inhale, draw in the moon's light and with each exhale, release tension and distractions.
3. **Light the Candle** Light the silver or white candle and say:
*"Moon so bright, full and wise,
Shine your light, open my eyes.*

*Reflect my thoughts, reveal what's true,
Illuminate my path, guide me through."*

4. **Focus on the Mirror** Hold the small mirror in your hands and angle it to reflect the moon's glow. Gaze into the mirror and let the light create a halo around your face. Visualize the moon's energy flowing from the mirror into your mind, clearing any mental fog and inviting deep introspection.
5. **Speak Your Intention** Whisper your intention or question into the moonlit space. For example: *"What truth do I need to see?"* or *"Show me the clarity I seek in my thoughts."* Feel the weight of your words traveling through the moonlight.
6. **Use the Bowl of Water** Dip your fingers into the bowl of water and touch your temples and heart, saying: *"By moon and water, clear and bright,
Reveal what's hidden in this night.
Wash away doubt, bring insight near,
Show me the path, make it clear."*

Close your eyes and let the cool touch of the water relax you. Visualize the moonlight blending with the water, purifying your thoughts and drawing out clarity.

1. **Write Your Reflections** Open your eyes and take the pen and paper. Write down any thoughts, feelings, or images that come to you. Be open to whatever surfaces, even if it feels vague or incomplete at first. The act of writing helps to translate subconscious messages into conscious understanding.
2. **Meditate with the Crystal** Hold the moonstone or selenite crystal in your hand or place it on your third eye (forehead). Meditate for a few minutes, focusing on your breath and the flow of moonlight. Allow insights to emerge naturally without force. The crystal will amplify the energy and guide your intuition.

3. **Seal the Ritual** To conclude the ritual, look back into the mirror and say: *"Moon above, I thank your light,*
For the guidance and the sight.
With this clarity, I am whole,
Balanced mind and steady soul."

Blow out the candle and express gratitude to the moon for its energy. Allow the candle to cool and store the mirror and crystal in a special place.

Post-Ritual Practices

- **Reflect on Your Notes:** In the days following the ritual, review your notes and see if any new thoughts or solutions come to mind. Often, clarity continues to unfold after the initial spell.
- **Keep the Mirror Close:** Use the mirror as a sacred tool in future rituals for reflection and clarity.
- **Moon Water for Future Use:** Leave the bowl of water in the moonlight overnight to create moon water. This can be used for future spells, cleansing, or as a soothing drink (if it's purified water) to maintain the energy of the full moon.

Enhancements for More Potency

- **Add Aromatherapy:** Burn lavender or sandalwood incense during the ritual to enhance relaxation and mental focus.
- **Chanting for Deepening:** Add a chant or mantra, such as *"Luna, guide me,"* throughout the ritual to maintain focus.
- **Use a Moon Journal:** Keep a special journal dedicated to your full moon reflections, making it easier to track patterns and realizations over time.

Practical Applications of the Spell

The *Moonlit Reflection Spell* is particularly helpful when facing major life decisions, personal growth challenges, or when seeking to understand emotions and relationships more deeply. By aligning with the full moon's energy, you can achieve a state of heightened awareness and insight, allowing you to move forward with greater confidence and understanding.

Embrace the full moon's power and let its light illuminate your inner world. With the clarity gained from this spell, you can approach life's challenges with newfound insight and balance.

Chapter 6: The Shield of Thorns
A spell for personal protection using natural elements

Introduction to the Spell

In times of uncertainty or when facing negativity, it is essential to create a protective barrier that shields you from harm while allowing you to move forward with confidence. The *Shield of Thorns* spell draws upon the symbolic and physical properties of natural elements to form an energy shield that deflects negative influences and keeps your personal energy safe. Inspired by the protective nature of thorny plants like rose bushes and brambles, this spell harnesses their defensive qualities to create a resilient barrier around you.

This spell is ideal for those who want to guard against unwanted energies, toxic influences, or even psychic disturbances. By weaving together the properties of nature's thorns, you invoke a powerful natural defense system that offers both spiritual and psychological protection.

The Symbolism of Thorns

Thorns have been used throughout history as symbols of resilience and protection. They represent a natural defense mechanism, capable of warding off predators while preserving the beauty and vitality of what they protect. In magic, thorns are associated with the ability to create boundaries, repel negativity, and maintain personal strength. This spell utilizes the thorn's essence to form an invisible yet potent barrier that surrounds and shields you.

Ideal Timing and Preparations

- **Best Time for the Ritual:** This spell can be performed at any time but is particularly potent during the waning moon, a phase known for banishing and protective work. It can also be enhanced by performing it at dusk, symbolizing the shift from light to protective shadow.
- **Location:** A quiet outdoor space surrounded by nature is ideal, but an indoor space with natural elements will suffice.

- **Mindset:** Approach this ritual with a firm intention to protect yourself and maintain your personal boundaries.

Materials Needed

- A small bundle of thorny branches (rose, hawthorn, or bramble are ideal)
- A black or dark green candle (for protection)
- Salt or a circle of protective herbs (e.g., rosemary, sage)
- A small piece of paper and a pen
- Essential oil such as cedarwood or frankincense (for anointing)
- A protective crystal such as black tourmaline or obsidian
- A bowl of water

The Ritual: Step-by-Step Guide

1. **Prepare Your Space** Set up your space by creating a protective circle. Sprinkle salt or arrange protective herbs around your ritual area to form a boundary. Place the candle in the center, surrounded by the thorny branches. Have your crystal and bowl of water nearby.
2. **Ground and Center** Sit comfortably in the center of your circle. Close your eyes and take deep, steady breaths. Visualize roots extending from your body into the earth, anchoring you securely. With each inhale, imagine drawing up the earth's grounding energy; with each exhale, release tension and any sense of vulnerability.
3. **Anoint and Light the Candle** Anoint the black or dark green candle with a few drops of cedarwood or frankincense essential oil while focusing on your intention for protection. Light the candle and say: *"Flame of the forest, strong and bold,*
Guard my spirit, as thorns unfold.

Create a shield, safe and warm,
Encircle me in nature's arm."

4. **Create the Shield of Thorns** Hold the thorny branches in your hands and focus on their protective energy. Visualize them forming an impenetrable circle around you, weaving together into a barrier that keeps out negativity and harm. Chant: *"Thorns of rose, thorns of might,*
Form a shield, sharp and tight.
Keep away what seeks me ill,
Protect my heart, protect my will."

5. **Set Your Intention** On the piece of paper, write down your specific intention for protection. For example: *"I am protected from negative energy and harmful intentions."* Fold the paper and place it under the candle, allowing the flame to infuse it with power.

6. **Infuse the Water with Energy** Dip your fingers into the bowl of water and lightly sprinkle it around the circle, saying: *"Water, gentle yet profound,*
Strengthen this shield all around.
Guard me well, day and night,
Keep me safe, keep me in light."

Imagine the water activating the boundary of thorns, making it stronger and more vibrant.

1. **Empower with the Crystal** Hold the protective crystal in your dominant hand and close your eyes. Visualize the crystal's energy merging with the shield of thorns, amplifying its power and solidity. Say: *"Stone of strength, stone of guard,*
Join this circle, make it hard.
Shield me from what may come,
Till my will and strength are one."

Place the crystal at the edge of your circle or carry it with you for ongoing protection.

1. **Seal the Spell** Focus on the candle's flame and visualize it burning away any lingering doubts or fears. Say: *"By flame, by thorn, by earth and sea,*
My protection is cast, so mote it be."

Allow the candle to burn for as long as is safe, or extinguish it with gratitude.

Post-Ritual Practices

- **Carry the Crystal:** Keep the protective crystal in your pocket or wear it as jewelry for continued support.
- **Visualize the Shield:** Throughout your day, take a moment to visualize the shield of thorns around you when you need an extra boost of protection.
- **Renew the Ritual Monthly:** Revisit this ritual on a monthly basis or whenever you feel the need to strengthen your protective boundaries.

Enhancements for More Potency

- **Add Incense:** Burn protective incense such as dragon's blood or sandalwood during the ritual to enhance the spell's potency.
- **Protective Affirmations:** In the days following the ritual, repeat affirmations such as *"I am surrounded by a shield of strength and safety."*
- **Use a Protection Sigil:** Draw or carve a protection sigil on the candle before lighting it to amplify your intention.

Practical Applications of the Spell

The *Shield of Thorns* spell is perfect for times when you need an added layer of protection, whether due to work stress, emotional strain, or exposure to negative environments. It can be performed before important events, when facing challenging situations, or whenever you feel the need for spiritual and emotional reinforcement.

By invoking the essence of nature's thorns, you create a strong, resilient shield that guards your personal energy and well-being. This spell taps into the wisdom of the earth and the innate power of natural defenses, allowing you to move through life protected, strong, and surrounded by the energies of safety and resilience.

Chapter 7: The Blossom of Friendship Spell

A unique spell to foster deep and lasting friendships

Introduction to the Spell

Friendship is one of life's most treasured relationships, providing support, joy, and a sense of belonging. Whether you wish to strengthen existing bonds or attract new, meaningful connections, the *Blossom of Friendship Spell* is designed to foster deep and lasting friendships. This ritual uses the energy of blossoms, herbs, and symbolic items to cultivate warmth, trust, and loyalty. By drawing upon the nurturing essence of nature, this spell helps you surround yourself with people who uplift and inspire you.

Friendships, like flowers, thrive when given attention, care, and the right conditions. This spell taps into those principles, inviting an energy of connection that blossoms into lifelong companionships.

Symbolism of Blossoms in Magic

Blossoms have long been symbols of growth, renewal, and beauty. They represent the unfolding of potential and the sharing of joy. In magical practice, different blossoms can signify love, friendship, and harmony, making them ideal for rituals focused on relationships. For this spell, blossoms are used as vessels of intention, carrying your desires for friendship into the world.

Ideal Timing and Preparations

- **Best Time for the Ritual:** This spell is best performed on a Friday, a day associated with Venus, the planet of love and relationships. It is especially powerful when done during the waxing moon, a time for growth and attraction.
- **Location:** A peaceful outdoor space, such as a garden, or an indoor space decorated with fresh flowers.

- **Mindset:** Approach this spell with an open heart, ready to welcome new connections and strengthen existing ones.

Materials Needed

- Fresh blossoms or flowers (roses, daisies, or any flower that symbolizes friendship)
- A pink or yellow candle (symbolizing friendship and joy)
- A bowl of spring or rose water
- Dried lavender or chamomile (for harmony and peace)
- A small piece of rose quartz or amethyst (to amplify loving and positive energy)
- A piece of paper and a pen
- A few drops of vanilla or jasmine essential oil (for inviting warmth)

The Ritual: Step-by-Step Guide

1. **Set Up Your Sacred Space** Choose a comfortable space for your ritual and arrange the flowers in a circle around you. Place the pink or yellow candle in the center, surrounded by the bowl of water and dried herbs. Anoint the candle with a few drops of vanilla or jasmine essential oil to infuse it with warmth and welcoming energy.
2. **Ground and Center** Sit comfortably with your spine straight and feet firmly on the ground. Close your eyes and take several deep breaths. Visualize roots extending from the base of your spine into the earth, anchoring you and connecting you to the energy of growth and renewal.
3. **Light the Candle** Light the candle and say: *"Candle bright, warm and kind,*
Bring to me friends of heart and mind.

*With your flame, bonds shall bloom,
Fill this space, dispel the gloom."*

4. **Infuse the Water** Sprinkle the dried lavender or chamomile into the bowl of water and gently swirl it clockwise three times. As you do this, imagine the water absorbing the harmonious and soothing properties of the herbs.
5. **Hold the Blossoms** Take the fresh blossoms in your hands and hold them close to your heart. Close your eyes and visualize yourself surrounded by kind, supportive, and joyful friends. Imagine laughter, shared experiences, and deep conversations. Feel the warmth and love that true friendship brings. Say: *"Blossoms of beauty, full and bright,
Bring true friends into my sight.
Let our bonds grow, strong and fair,
With trust, love, and care."*
6. **Write Your Intentions** On the piece of paper, write down your intentions for friendship. Be specific if you wish to strengthen an existing relationship or be more general if seeking new connections. For example: *"May I attract friends who bring joy, understanding, and mutual support."*
7. **Anoint the Paper** Dip your fingers into the bowl of water and lightly anoint the corners of the paper while saying: *"Water of harmony, herb of peace,
Let these friendships never cease.
As this paper absorbs your grace,
Bring me connections, heart to place."*

Fold the paper and place it under the candle, letting the flame infuse it with the energy of your intention.

1. **Invoke the Power of Crystals** Hold the rose quartz or amethyst in your hands and visualize its energy radiating warmth and positive vibrations. Say: *"Crystal clear, pure and true,*

Amplify my wish, as I ask of you.
Surround me with friends, loyal and bright,
Bring shared joy, both day and night."

Place the crystal next to the candle or keep it with you as a token of the spell.

1. **Conclude the Ritual** Close your eyes and take a final moment to feel the energy of the ritual. Visualize the blossoms opening, representing the new or strengthened friendships taking root in your life. Say: *"Thank you, blossoms, herbs, and light,*
For guiding my heart to what feels right.
Let friendship blossom, love abound,
In this sacred space, connections are found."

Extinguish the candle with gratitude and allow the water to rest overnight. You can use it to water a plant or sprinkle it outside the next day as a symbolic release of your intention.

Post-Ritual Practices

- **Carry the Crystal:** Keep the rose quartz or amethyst in your pocket or place it where you spend time to continue drawing in positive and friendly energy.
- **Fresh Flowers in Your Space:** Maintain fresh flowers in your living space as a reminder of the friendship spell and to keep the energy alive.
- **Mindful Actions:** Engage in activities that align with your intention, such as reaching out to friends, joining social groups, or attending community events.

Enhancements for More Potency

- **Use Incense:** Burn rose or sandalwood incense during the ritual to enhance the atmosphere of friendship and warmth.
- **Create a Friendship Talisman:** Place dried blossoms from the ritual into a small cloth pouch with the crystal to create a talisman you can carry with you.
- **Weekly Affirmations:** Repeat affirmations such as *"I am surrounded by loving and supportive friends"* to reinforce the spell's energy.

Practical Applications of the Spell

The *Blossom of Friendship Spell* is perfect for those looking to deepen their connections with existing friends or attract new, positive relationships into their lives. It's also useful when transitioning to a new environment, such as moving to a new city, starting a new job, or beginning school.

By inviting the energy of blossoms and nature's nurturing properties into your life, you create an environment where friendships can grow and thrive. This spell not only fosters strong connections but also aligns you with the energy of joy, understanding, and love, ensuring that your relationships are built on mutual respect and genuine care.

Chapter 8: Dewdrop Healing Charm

A practical charm using morning dew for physical and emotional healing

Introduction to the Spell

Morning dew has been revered for centuries as a symbol of purity, renewal, and the natural magic that dawn brings. Collected in the early hours when the world is still quiet and fresh, dew embodies the gentle, healing energy of the morning. The *Dewdrop Healing Charm* is designed to channel this energy for physical and emotional restoration. This ritual draws on the cleansing and nurturing properties of dew to soothe pain, refresh the spirit, and promote holistic healing.

Dew is known in folklore as "nature's elixir," believed to be infused with the vital essence of the earth and sky. By capturing this essence, you create a powerful tool that can be used to heal and rejuvenate the body and mind.

The Significance of Dew in Magic

Dew symbolizes new beginnings, purity, and the soft power of nature's renewal. It forms during the night as the earth cools and the moisture in the air condenses, gathering quietly on leaves, grass, and flowers. This subtle process of formation imbues dew with an almost mystical quality, making it a potent ingredient for charms and spells focused on healing, rejuvenation, and peace. In magical traditions, dew is associated with the elements of water and air, harmonizing emotions and promoting clarity.

Ideal Timing and Preparations

- **Best Time for the Ritual:** Perform this ritual at dawn, ideally on a clear day when dew is abundant and fresh.

- **Location:** A garden, park, or any natural space with plants that gather dew. If collecting dew outdoors isn't possible, place plants on a balcony or windowsill overnight to capture dew.
- **Mindset:** Approach the ritual with gratitude and an open heart, ready to receive the healing properties of nature.

Materials Needed

- A small, clean glass or crystal bowl for collecting dew
- A white cloth or silk handkerchief (to symbolize purity)
- A light blue or white candle (for peace and healing)
- A small piece of paper and a pen
- Dried chamomile or mint leaves (optional, for enhancing calmness)
- A rose quartz crystal (associated with love and healing)
- A small bottle or container with a cork (to store the dew)

The Ritual: Step-by-Step Guide

1. **Prepare Your Space** Begin by choosing a spot where you can collect dew at dawn. Arrange the candle, dried chamomile or mint leaves, and other materials near your chosen area. Place the glass bowl on the ground or among plants that naturally collect dew.
2. **Collect the Morning Dew** At first light, gather dew by gently brushing the white cloth or handkerchief over leaves, grass, or flower petals and wringing it into the glass bowl. As you collect the dew, say: *"Dew of dawn, pure and clear,*
Bring your healing essence here.
Earth and sky, combined so bright,
Infuse this charm with morning light."
3. **Ground and Center** Sit comfortably with the bowl of dew in front of you. Close your eyes and take a few deep breaths. Visualize roots extending from your body into the earth, grounding

you. With each breath, feel your connection to the earth's healing energy and the air's refreshing qualities.

4. **Light the Candle** Light the blue or white candle and say: *"Flame of peace, light of grace,*
Bless this water, bless this space.
Let healing flow, let spirits mend,
With this charm, may health ascend."
5. **Infuse with Intentions** Hold the rose quartz in your hands and focus on the area of your life or body that needs healing, whether it's physical pain, emotional distress, or mental fatigue. Say: *"Crystal of love, amplify,*
Healing energies, draw nigh.
Emotions calm, body restore,
Bring me peace forevermore."

Place the crystal beside the bowl of dew.

1. **Write Your Healing Intention** On the piece of paper, write down a short but clear statement of your healing intention. For example: *"May this dew bring comfort to my heart and rejuvenate my spirit."* Fold the paper and place it beneath the bowl.
2. **Enhance the Dew with Herbs (Optional)** Sprinkle a pinch of dried chamomile or mint leaves into the dew to amplify its calming and restorative properties. Gently stir the dew with your finger three times clockwise, visualizing the water absorbing the healing power of the herbs.
3. **Anoint Yourself with the Dew** Dip your fingers into the bowl and lightly touch your forehead, heart, and any areas of your body that need healing. As you do, say: *"Dew so pure, dew so light,*
Bring your strength both day and night.
With each touch, my health renew,
Body and spirit, fresh and true."

Feel the cool touch of the dew spreading a wave of relaxation and renewal through your body.

1. **Seal the Charm** Pour the remaining dew into the small bottle or container and cork it tightly. This dew-infused charm can be used for anointing during future moments of stress or when you need a boost of healing energy. As you seal the bottle, say: *"In this bottle, essence stays,*
Healing power for future days.
Guard and keep, protect and mend,
A charm of nature, a constant friend."
2. **Close the Ritual** Extinguish the candle with gratitude, saying:
"Thank you, dawn, for your gift so rare,
For your light, for your care.
Healing waters, sacred and true,
My thanks I give, my heart renew."

Post-Ritual Practices

- **Store the Dew Charm:** Keep the bottled dew in a cool, dark place. It can be used for future anointing or added to baths for continued healing benefits.
- **Daily Reflection:** Spend a few minutes each morning or evening reflecting on your healing journey. Use the dew charm as needed, touching your pulse points or your heart while visualizing the healing energy.
- **Repeat as Needed:** This ritual can be repeated monthly or as needed to refresh the charm and reinforce your healing process.

Enhancements for More Potency

- **Aromatherapy Addition:** Diffuse calming essential oils like lavender or eucalyptus during the ritual to enhance the soothing atmosphere.
- **Music for Relaxation:** Play soft, meditative music or nature sounds in the background to deepen your sense of peace.
- **Moonlit Dew Collection:** For added power, collect dew during a full moon to combine the moon's energy with the morning's purity.

Practical Applications of the Spell

The *Dewdrop Healing Charm* is particularly effective for periods of stress, illness, or emotional upheaval. It can also be used to start each day with a sense of calm and renewal. The charm is gentle yet powerful, making it suitable for people of all ages and for those who seek holistic approaches to well-being.

By using the pure energy of morning dew and combining it with natural elements and heartfelt intentions, you create a healing tool that supports your body and spirit. Let this charm remind you of nature's quiet strength and its capacity to soothe and mend.

Chapter 9: The Songbird's Fortune Call
A spell to attract positive news and opportunities

Introduction to the Spell

In times when life feels stagnant or when you seek positive change, opportunities, or good news, the *Songbird's Fortune Call* spell can help shift the winds of fate in your favor. Birds have long been seen as messengers of hope, joy, and transformation in various cultures and spiritual traditions. The melodious songs of birds, especially in the early morning, carry an energy that embodies freedom, renewal, and prosperity. This spell harnesses the songbird's natural power to call in opportunities and good tidings.

Drawing upon the spirit of birds and their connection to the element of air, this spell creates an open channel through which positive energy can flow into your life. It is especially effective for those seeking career breakthroughs, unexpected good news, or life-changing opportunities.

The Symbolism of Songbirds in Magic

Songbirds symbolize communication, change, and the arrival of new beginnings. Their cheerful songs at dawn signal hope and herald a fresh start. In magical practices, they are associated with the element of air, which governs intellect, communication, and the ability to receive and transmit messages. The songbird's call is believed to carry intentions to the universe, summoning abundance, good fortune, and favorable outcomes.

Ideal Timing and Preparations

- **Best Time for the Ritual:** Perform this spell at dawn, when birds are most active and their songs fill the air. The energy at this time is potent for calling in new opportunities.

- **Moon Phase:** The waxing or full moon is ideal for spells focused on growth and attraction.
- **Location:** An outdoor space where you can hear birdsong is perfect. If this isn't possible, an open window or a recording of birdsong can be used.
- **Mindset:** Approach this ritual with a sense of anticipation and openness, ready to welcome positive changes.

Materials Needed

- A feather (preferably one found in nature, symbolizing freedom and communication)
- A small, clear bell or wind chime (to mimic birdsong)
- A yellow or light blue candle (for optimism and clarity)
- Dried sunflower petals or marigold (for joy and good luck)
- A small piece of citrine or jade (for prosperity and opportunity)
- A piece of paper and a pen
- A bowl of spring water

The Ritual: Step-by-Step Guide

1. **Create Your Sacred Space** Set up your ritual space in an area where the first light of dawn can reach you. Place the candle in the center and arrange the feather, bell or wind chime, dried petals, and crystal around it. Ensure the bowl of spring water is within easy reach.
2. **Ground and Center** Stand or sit comfortably with your feet on the ground. Close your eyes and take several deep, calming breaths. Visualize roots extending from the soles of your feet deep into the earth, anchoring you. With each inhale, imagine drawing up the earth's energy; with each exhale, release any worries or stagnant energy.

3. **Light the Candle** Light the yellow or light blue candle and say:
   "Candle bright, flame so true,
   Bring fortune's light, fresh and new.
   With this flame, my call I send,
   Positive change, on you I depend."
4. **Infuse the Water** Sprinkle the dried sunflower petals or marigold into the bowl of water, infusing it with their bright, uplifting energy. Stir gently three times clockwise, visualizing the water absorbing the energy of joy and opportunity.
5. **Invoke the Songbird's Spirit** Hold the feather in your hands and close your eyes. Imagine the songbird's call echoing through the air, carrying your intention to the winds. Say: *"Bird of song, bird of flight,*
   Call my fortune, make it bright.
   Bring me news, opportunities,
   Let life's blessings come with ease."

Wave the feather gently through the air, as if mimicking the motion of a bird in flight.

1. **Ring the Bell or Wind Chime** Ring the bell or shake the wind chime lightly to create a sound reminiscent of birdsong. This sound acts as a carrier for your intentions, sending them into the universe. As the sound resonates, say: *"With every note, with every ring,*
   Fortune, come, on whispered wing.
   Good news fly, new paths unfold,
   Let life's wonders now be told."
2. **Write Your Intention** On the piece of paper, write down your specific desire for opportunities or good news. Be clear and concise, such as *"I welcome new opportunities and positive change into my life."* Fold the paper and place it beneath the candle.

3. **Empower with the Crystal** Hold the citrine or jade in your hands, infusing it with your intention for prosperity and good fortune. Visualize the crystal glowing with a warm, golden light. Say: *"Stone of fortune, stone so bright,*
Amplify this wish tonight.
Let good news and chances near,
Come to me, loud and clear."

Place the crystal next to the candle or carry it with you as a token of the spell.

1. **Anoint Yourself** Dip your fingers into the infused water and touch your forehead and heart, saying: *"Dew of dawn, sun's first glow,*
Bring me chances, let blessings flow."
2. **Close the Ritual** Extinguish the candle with gratitude, saying: *"Thank you, songbird, air, and light,*
For bringing fortune, pure and bright.
May my call be heard far and wide,
As I trust in fate's gentle tide."

Post-Ritual Practices

- **Carry the Feather or Crystal:** Keep the feather or crystal with you as a reminder of the spell and a talisman of opportunity.
- **Listen for Birdsong:** Pay attention to birdsong throughout the day or the following days. Use it as a cue to remind yourself that good news and opportunities are on their way.
- **Refresh the Spell Monthly:** Repeat this ritual on a monthly basis or whenever you feel the need to attract positive energy and new opportunities.

Enhancements for More Potency

- **Add Aromatherapy:** Burn a stick of lemongrass or sandalwood incense during the ritual to enhance the uplifting and inviting atmosphere.
- **Use Affirmations:** Repeat affirmations such as *"I am open to receiving new and positive opportunities"* in the days following the ritual.
- **Sunrise Visualization:** Visualize a sunrise each morning to reinforce the spell's energy and invite new beginnings.

Practical Applications of the Spell

The *Songbird's Fortune Call* spell is perfect for anyone who feels stuck or is waiting for a positive change in life, whether in career, relationships, or personal growth. It can be used before important interviews, when awaiting news, or during times of transition when you need a little push from the universe.

By invoking the cheerful and free-spirited energy of the songbird, you align yourself with the air's currents of communication and change. This spell helps open channels for positive energy and opportunities to flow, bringing you closer to the life you desire. Trust in the songbird's call, and let its song guide your journey to fortune and joy.

Chapter 10: Twilight Dream Enchantment

A ritual to enhance lucid dreaming and intuitive visions

Introduction to the Spell

Dreams have long been a source of inspiration, insight, and spiritual guidance. They bridge the gap between the conscious and subconscious mind, offering a window into deeper truths and hidden knowledge. The *Twilight Dream Enchantment* ritual is designed to enhance lucid dreaming and open the mind to intuitive visions. By performing this ritual, you prepare yourself to navigate the dream world with awareness, unlocking insights and guidance that can illuminate your waking life.

This ritual uses the transitional energy of twilight—a time that blends day and night—to amplify your intuitive abilities. Twilight is considered a liminal space, a powerful moment when the boundaries between worlds blur, making it the perfect time to harness dream magic and increase your potential for lucid dreaming.

The Significance of Twilight in Magic

Twilight, the brief time between daylight and nightfall, holds a unique energy that is neither fully of the light nor the dark. It represents transformation, mystery, and the in-between—a state where hidden truths and subconscious insights come to the surface. In magical practices, twilight is a time for reflection, divination, and connection with the deeper layers of existence. This spell taps into twilight's transformative energy to enhance your ability to dream lucidly and receive intuitive visions.

Ideal Timing and Preparations

- **Best Time for the Ritual:** Perform this spell during the twilight hours, just after sunset and before night fully sets in.

- **Moon Phase:** The full moon or waxing moon is ideal for enhancing intuitive powers and dream work.
- **Location:** A quiet, dimly lit space where you can be undisturbed. Ideally, near a window where you can see the fading light of dusk.
- **Mindset:** Approach the ritual with an open mind and a sense of wonder. Prepare yourself to explore the realm of dreams with intention and awareness.

Materials Needed

- A deep blue or purple candle (for intuition and dreamwork)
- Dried lavender or mugwort (known for enhancing dreams and intuition)
- A small bowl of moon-charged water or spring water
- A piece of amethyst or lapis lazuli (for enhancing psychic abilities)
- A journal and pen (for recording dreams and visions)
- A soft cloth or eye mask
- A small mirror (optional, for deeper vision work)
- A few drops of sandalwood or jasmine essential oil

The Ritual: Step-by-Step Guide

1. **Create Your Sacred Space** Arrange your ritual space so that the candle sits in the center. Surround it with the dried lavender or mugwort, the bowl of water, and the amethyst or lapis lazuli. If you're using the optional mirror, place it behind the candle so it reflects the flame's light.
2. **Ground and Center** Sit comfortably with your feet touching the floor or the ground. Close your eyes and take a series of slow, deep breaths. Visualize roots growing from your body, connecting you to the earth below. With each breath, feel yourself becoming more grounded and present in the moment.

3. **Light the Candle** Light the deep blue or purple candle and say:
   "Twilight hour, soft and deep,
   Bring the visions as I sleep.
   Open doors, lift the veil,
   Let dreams be clear, let wisdom prevail."
4. **Anoint Your Temples** Apply a few drops of sandalwood or jasmine essential oil to your temples and wrists. The calming, fragrant scent will help open your mind and prepare you for the dream world. Say: *"Scent of the sacred, guide me within,*
   To dreams that heal and truths that begin."
5. **Infuse the Water with Intention** Gently stir the moon-charged water with your finger while focusing on your intention. Whisper into the water: *"Water of moon, water of night,*
   Carry my dreams, guide my sight."

Use a few drops of this water to anoint your forehead, enhancing your third eye's receptivity to intuitive visions.

1. **Hold the Crystal** Take the amethyst or lapis lazuli in your dominant hand. Close your eyes and visualize a violet or indigo light flowing from the crystal into your body, stimulating your mind and enhancing your connection to the dream realm. Say: *"Crystal of insight, stone of dreams,*
   Open the gates, let visions stream.
   I seek the wisdom, I seek the guide,
   Let dreams be lucid, let truths reside."
2. **Gaze into the Candle's Flame** Spend a few moments focusing on the candle's flame. Allow your mind to relax as you gaze, letting your thoughts drift. This is a meditative moment to prepare your subconscious mind for dreaming. If using the mirror, glance at the reflection of the flame to deepen your sense of introspection.

3. **Set Your Dream Intention** On a piece of paper, write your intention for your dreamwork. For example: *"Tonight, I will dream lucidly and receive clear guidance on [your topic or question]."* Place this paper under the candle.
4. **Anoint the Eye Mask or Cloth** Dab a small amount of the moon-charged water or essential oil onto the soft cloth or eye mask. This will serve as a final signal to your subconscious that it's time to enter the dream world. Say: *"By the cloth of night, I close my eyes,*
Enter dreams where truth lies.
Guide my spirit, clear and bright,
Grant me visions through this night."
5. **Close the Ritual** Extinguish the candle with gratitude, saying: *"Twilight's blessing, dreams so rare,*
Guide my sleep with tender care.
From dusk till dawn, let visions play,
And bring insight come the day."

Post-Ritual Practices

- **Sleep with the Crystal:** Place the amethyst or lapis lazuli under your pillow or on your nightstand to maintain the spell's energy.
- **Record Your Dreams:** Keep the journal and pen by your bed. As soon as you wake up, write down any dreams or visions you remember. This helps capture details that might fade quickly after waking.
- **Reflect on Your Dreams:** Review your dream notes and look for patterns, symbols, or messages. Intuitive insights often come through symbolism, so trust your instincts when interpreting your dreams.

Enhancements for More Potency

- **Background Music:** Play soft, ambient music or nature sounds to create an even more relaxing atmosphere.
- **Use Herbal Sachets:** Place a small sachet filled with dried lavender or mugwort under your pillow to deepen the dream state.
- **Repeat Affirmations:** Before going to sleep, repeat affirmations such as *"I am open to receiving clear and powerful dreams tonight."*

Practical Applications of the Spell

The *Twilight Dream Enchantment* spell is particularly useful for those seeking answers to life's questions, emotional clarity, or creative inspiration. It can be performed as part of a nightly routine or during specific times when you need guidance and insight. This spell is also effective when used in conjunction with other divinatory practices like tarot or scrying to deepen understanding.

By attuning yourself to the energy of twilight and harnessing its connection to dreams and visions, you create a pathway for enhanced intuitive abilities and the potential for lucid dreaming. Let the dream world reveal its mysteries and guide you with wisdom and insight that transcends the waking mind. Embrace the gift of dreaming and use its messages to illuminate your journey.

Chapter 11: The Oak's Strength Invocation
A spell to borrow the strength and resilience of ancient oaks

Introduction to the Spell

The oak tree has stood as a symbol of strength, resilience, and wisdom throughout the ages. Revered in numerous cultures and mythologies, the oak embodies fortitude and stability, qualities needed when facing life's challenges. The *Oak's Strength Invocation* is a powerful ritual designed to help you draw on the essence of the oak's enduring nature to bolster your inner strength and resilience. This spell channels the steady, grounded energy of the oak tree, empowering you to stand firm in the face of adversity, overcome obstacles, and maintain unwavering confidence.

By connecting with the deep-rooted energy of the oak, you create a bridge to the earth's strength and gain the fortitude to weather life's storms. This ritual can be used in times of personal struggle, when preparing for a difficult task, or whenever you need to reinforce your spirit with the power of nature.

The Symbolism of the Oak in Magic

The oak is often regarded as the "King of Trees," symbolizing power, stability, and endurance. Its deep roots and towering branches represent a connection between the heavens and the earth, making it a sacred tree in Druidic, Celtic, Norse, and other traditions. The oak's acorns are seen as tokens of potential and growth, while the tree itself is viewed as a guardian and protector. Harnessing the energy of the oak can instill a profound sense of resilience and strength in your own spirit.

Ideal Timing and Preparations

- **Best Time for the Ritual:** This ritual is best performed on a Sunday (associated with the Sun, symbolizing strength and vital-

ity) or on the day of the full moon for added power. Dawn or midday are ideal times for invoking the strength of the oak.
- **Location:** Outdoors near an oak tree is perfect, but if that isn't possible, an indoor space with oak leaves, branches, or acorns will suffice.
- **Mindset:** Approach this ritual with a sense of respect and reverence for nature. Be ready to embrace the power of the oak and channel its energy into your being.

Materials Needed

- A small piece of oak wood, an acorn, or an oak leaf
- A green or brown candle (to represent the forest and earth)
- A bowl of earth or soil (to ground the ritual)
- A stone or crystal associated with strength, such as hematite or tiger's eye
- A piece of paper and a pen
- Cedar or frankincense incense (optional, for grounding and strength)
- A small cup of herbal tea (such as oak bark or chamomile, optional for reflection)

The Ritual: Step-by-Step Guide

1. **Prepare Your Sacred Space** If outdoors, find a spot near an oak tree where you can sit comfortably. If indoors, place the oak wood, acorn, or oak leaf in the center of your ritual space. Surround it with the candle, bowl of earth, and crystal. Light the cedar or frankincense incense to create a calming, earthy atmosphere.
2. **Ground and Center** Stand or sit with your feet flat on the ground. Close your eyes and take deep breaths, visualizing roots growing from the soles of your feet deep into the earth, inter-

twining with the roots of the great oaks. Feel the earth's stabilizing energy moving up through these roots and into your body, grounding and centering you.

3. **Light the Candle** Light the green or brown candle and say:
"Candle of earth, flame so bright,
Guide my spirit with your light.
With oak's strength, I call to thee,
Grant me power, steadfast and free."

4. **Hold the Oak Symbol** Take the piece of oak wood, acorn, or leaf in your hands and close your eyes. Imagine the oak tree, its massive branches stretching skyward and its roots gripping the earth firmly. Feel the energy of this ancient tree flowing into you through your hands. Say: *"Mighty oak, strong and wise,*
Share your strength, let it rise.
Rooted deep, standing tall,
Grant me power, unyielding to all."

5. **Infuse the Earth with Your Intention** Sprinkle some of the earth or soil over the oak symbol while envisioning your intention merging with the grounding power of the earth. Say: *"Earth below, solid and strong,*
Bind me to strength where I belong.
Let my spirit be firm as stone,
Rooted, resilient, never alone."

6. **Empower with the Crystal** Hold the hematite or tiger's eye in your dominant hand and visualize a radiant light emanating from the crystal, weaving through your body and infusing every cell with strength and determination. Say: *"Stone of power, earth's own core,*
Empower me, let courage soar.
With every breath, strength renew,
I am oak, steadfast and true."

7. **Write Your Affirmation** On the piece of paper, write down an affirmation that embodies the strength you wish to draw from

this ritual. For example: *"I am as strong and unyielding as the mighty oak. I stand firm in my truth and overcome all challenges."* Place the paper under the bowl of earth to symbolize grounding your intention.

8. **Visualize the Energy** Sit in silence for a few moments, holding the oak symbol and crystal close to your heart. Visualize the energy of the oak enveloping you like a protective, powerful aura. Imagine yourself standing tall like the oak, unbending in the face of any challenge.
9. **Conclude the Ritual** Extinguish the candle and say: *"Thank you, oak, for strength bestowed,*
For resilience and the courage showed.
Earth and flame, crystal bright,
I am empowered, day and night."

Post-Ritual Practices

- **Carry the Oak Symbol or Crystal:** Keep the piece of oak wood, acorn, or crystal with you as a talisman of strength.
- **Affirm Daily:** Repeat the affirmation you wrote each morning to reinforce the energy of the spell.
- **Reconnect with Nature:** Spend time outdoors, especially around oak trees, to maintain your connection with this source of power.

Enhancements for More Potency

- **Meditate by an Oak Tree:** Enhance the ritual's energy by meditating near an oak tree regularly.
- **Wear Green or Brown:** Incorporate these colors into your clothing or accessories as reminders of the ritual's energy.
- **Drink Oak Bark Tea:** Reflect with a cup of oak bark tea to embody the essence of the oak internally.

Practical Applications of the Spell

The *Oak's Strength Invocation* spell is especially useful during times of personal upheaval, before facing a significant challenge, or when you need to bolster your confidence and resilience. This spell empowers you to handle adversity with grace, remain grounded, and maintain a strong sense of self no matter what life throws your way.

By channeling the enduring energy of the oak, you align yourself with centuries of resilience and strength. The power of this ritual remains with you, a quiet force that helps you weather life's storms and stand unyielding, rooted, and confident. Embrace the strength of the oak and let it guide you through every challenge with unwavering resolve.

Chapter 12: The Herb Weaver's Prosperity Knot
A prosperity spell involving herb bundles and simple knot magic

Introduction to the Spell

Prosperity is a multifaceted concept that encompasses not only financial wealth but also abundance in opportunities, relationships, and well-being. The *Herb Weaver's Prosperity Knot* spell is designed to attract this holistic form of prosperity using the combined power of herbs and knot magic. This ritual weaves together the energies of specific prosperity-enhancing herbs into a bundle that is secured with knots, symbolizing the binding of abundance to your life.

Knot magic is one of the oldest forms of spellwork, known for its simplicity and effectiveness. It allows the practitioner to focus intention into each knot, solidifying desires and wishes in a tangible way. By incorporating the power of herbs, which carry their own unique vibrations and properties, this spell harnesses the forces of nature to invite prosperity into your life.

The Symbolism of Herbs and Knot Magic

Herbs have been used for millennia in magical practices due to their potent natural energies. Specific herbs like basil, cinnamon, and bay leaves are known for their associations with prosperity, success, and wealth. Knot magic, on the other hand, embodies the power of intention through the act of tying and binding. Each knot represents the securing of a wish, holding energy until it is released or manifests.

By combining these two elements, the spell creates a powerful tool for attracting prosperity and abundance into your life.

Ideal Timing and Preparations

- **Best Time for the Ritual:** This spell is best performed on a Thursday (associated with Jupiter, the planet of growth and abundance) or during a waxing moon, which is a time for attracting and drawing in prosperity.

- **Location:** A quiet space where you can work without interruption. Outdoors in a garden or near plants would be ideal for connecting with nature.
- **Mindset:** Approach this ritual with a clear intention and belief in your ability to attract prosperity. Feel a sense of gratitude as if your desires have already been fulfilled.

Materials Needed

- A green or gold cord or ribbon (for prosperity and wealth)
- A small bundle of herbs such as basil, cinnamon sticks, and bay leaves (all associated with prosperity)
- A piece of paper and a pen
- Essential oil such as patchouli or bergamot (for enhancing abundance)
- A small cloth pouch or piece of fabric to hold the herb bundle
- A green candle (for attracting prosperity)
- A bowl of salt (for purification)

The Ritual: Step-by-Step Guide

1. **Prepare Your Sacred Space** Begin by setting up your ritual space. Place the green candle in the center and surround it with the bowl of salt, the herbs, the cord or ribbon, and the cloth pouch. Anoint the candle with a few drops of patchouli or bergamot essential oil to amplify its energy for abundance.
2. **Purify the Space** Sprinkle salt around your space to cleanse it of any negative energy. As you do this, say: *"Salt of earth, pure and bright,*
Guard this space with your light.
Clear away what does not serve,
Make way for blessings I deserve."

3. **Ground and Center** Sit comfortably with your feet on the ground. Close your eyes, take deep breaths, and visualize roots growing from your body into the earth, anchoring you and connecting you to its abundant energy. Feel grounded, present, and ready to weave prosperity into your life.
4. **Light the Candle** Light the green candle and say: *"Flame of fortune, glow so bright,*
Draw prosperity into my sight.
Let abundance come, swift and true,
As I will it, so it shall ensue."
5. **Prepare the Herb Bundle** Take the basil, cinnamon sticks, and bay leaves, and place them in the center of the cloth. Visualize each herb radiating energy as you hold it:
    - **Basil** for financial success and harmony
    - **Cinnamon** for swift luck and positive energy
    - **Bay leaves** for wishes and manifesting prosperity

Say: *"Herbs of wealth, herbs of might,*
Bring prosperity, day and night.
Infuse this bundle with your grace,
Attract abundance to this place."

1. **Write Your Intention** On the piece of paper, write a concise statement of your intention. For example: *"I attract wealth, opportunities, and success into my life."* Fold the paper and place it in the herb bundle.
2. **Create the Prosperity Knot** Take the cord or ribbon and begin tying knots around the herb bundle. With each knot, repeat your intention out loud or in your mind. For example:
    - **First Knot:** "I bind prosperity to my path."
    - **Second Knot:** "I secure abundance in all I do."
    - **Third Knot:** "I call forth opportunities, bright and true."

Continue until you have tied a total of three, five, or nine knots (numbers associated with growth, power, and completion).

1. **Anoint the Bundle** Anoint the herb bundle lightly with the essential oil, infusing it with the scent and energy of abundance. Say: *"Oil of richness, scent so fine,*
Bless this charm, make it mine.
Prosperity bound, held within,
Let success and fortune begin."
2. **Empower the Bundle with Candlelight** Hold the herb bundle over the flame (at a safe distance) and visualize the flame's energy infusing the bundle with warmth and light. Say: *"By fire's glow, this charm I bless,*
Bring wealth and joy, no more, no less.
Flame and herb, cord and might,
Prosperity flows with this rite."
3. **Seal the Intention** Place the herb bundle into the cloth pouch and tie it securely. Extinguish the candle with gratitude and say: *"Thank you, flame, thank you, earth,*
For this spell and its rebirth.
Blessings come, abundance near,
Prosperity grows, free from fear."

Post-Ritual Practices

- **Keep the Charm Close:** Carry the pouch with you, place it in your workspace, or keep it on your altar to continuously draw prosperity into your life.
- **Reinforce the Spell Weekly:** Hold the charm and repeat your intention once a week to maintain its energy.
- **Use Affirmations:** Reinforce the spell's power by saying affirmations such as *"I am open to receiving the prosperity that flows into my life."* daily.

Enhancements for More Potency

- **Add Citrine or Green Aventurine:** Include a small piece of citrine or green aventurine in the pouch for extra amplification of wealth and success.
- **Burn Prosperity Incense:** Burn incense like myrrh, frankincense, or cinnamon while holding the charm to further enhance the spell's power.
- **Visualization Practice:** Spend a few minutes each day visualizing your life filled with the prosperity you seek.

Practical Applications of the Spell

The *Herb Weaver's Prosperity Knot* spell is perfect for times when you need financial stability, are starting a new venture, or wish to bring more abundance into various aspects of your life. It can be used before important meetings, when launching new projects, or during periods of economic uncertainty.

By combining the potent energies of herbs and knot magic, this spell serves as a beacon that calls prosperity to your life. It connects you to the nurturing power of nature and the focused intention of your own will, ensuring that abundance is not just hoped for but actively woven into your reality. Let this charm be a constant reminder that you have the power to create and sustain prosperity, no matter where life leads you.

Chapter 13: Crystal Pool Purification

A spell for personal cleansing and renewal using reflective water and crystals

Introduction to the Spell

Throughout history, water has been regarded as one of the most powerful elements for purification, renewal, and healing. When combined with the transformative energy of crystals, water becomes a potent tool for personal cleansing and spiritual rejuvenation. The *Crystal Pool Purification* spell is designed to wash away negative energy, release emotional burdens, and restore a sense of balance and clarity. By using reflective water and specific crystals, this ritual taps into the harmonizing qualities of both elements to cleanse the body, mind, and spirit.

This spell is ideal for moments when you feel weighed down by stress, emotional heaviness, or a buildup of negative energy. It can be performed after a challenging period, during times of personal transformation, or simply as a routine practice for maintaining energetic hygiene.

The Symbolism of Water and Crystals in Magic

Water is symbolic of life, intuition, emotion, and the subconscious. It has the power to cleanse, renew, and connect us with the depths of our inner world. Reflective water, in particular, mirrors our thoughts and emotions, allowing us to release what no longer serves us and welcome what we need for healing and growth.

Crystals, on the other hand, are natural conduits of energy, each carrying unique properties that can amplify, cleanse, or balance our vibrations. When paired with water, crystals enhance the healing process by directing energy and intentions, creating a harmonious flow that revitalizes the soul.

Ideal Timing and Preparations

- **Best Time for the Ritual:** This spell is most effective during a full moon, when the moon's energy is at its peak and can infuse

the water with cleansing properties. It can also be performed during a waxing moon for rejuvenation and growth.
- **Location:** Near a natural water source such as a river, lake, or pond is ideal, but an indoor space with a large bowl of water or a small pool can be used.
- **Mindset:** Approach this ritual with the intention of release and renewal. Be open to letting go of negativity and embracing a refreshed state of mind.

Materials Needed

- A large bowl or basin of spring or moon-charged water
- A reflective surface or mirror (optional, for focusing intentions)
- Crystals such as clear quartz, amethyst, and selenite (for purification and clarity)
- Fresh rosemary or mint leaves (for added cleansing properties)
- A white or blue candle (for purity and tranquility)
- A small piece of paper and a pen
- Essential oil such as eucalyptus or lavender (optional for relaxation)
- A soft cloth or towel

The Ritual: Step-by-Step Guide

1. **Prepare Your Sacred Space** Set up your ritual space in a quiet location where you can be undisturbed. Place the bowl or basin of water in the center and surround it with the crystals, candle, and fresh herbs. If using a reflective surface or mirror, position it so it reflects the water. Anoint the candle with a few drops of essential oil to infuse it with a calming energy.
2. **Cleanse the Space** Light the candle and say: *"Candle of light, pure and bright,*
Cleanse this space, day or night.

*Let peace flow, let calm preside,
Wash away what's dark inside."*

Allow the flame to flicker, creating a serene and sacred atmosphere.

1. **Ground and Center** Stand or sit comfortably with your feet on the ground. Close your eyes and take deep, steady breaths. Visualize roots extending from your body into the earth, grounding you and connecting you to the stabilizing force of the earth. With each inhale, feel yourself becoming more present and anchored.
2. **Infuse the Water with Herbs** Add the fresh rosemary or mint leaves to the bowl of water. As you do, imagine the water becoming infused with the cleansing energy of the herbs. Say: *"Herbs of purity, herbs of green,
Cleanse this water, keep it serene.
By nature's gift, by moon's delight,
Bring renewal, clear my sight."*
3. **Empower the Water with Crystals** Gently place the clear quartz, amethyst, and selenite into the water. Visualize each crystal releasing its energy into the water, creating ripples of light and purification. Say: *"Crystals of clarity, crystals so pure,
Infuse this water with a cleansing cure.
Let your light, your power blend,
Cleanse my spirit, let healing ascend."*
4. **Set Your Intention** On the piece of paper, write a brief statement of what you wish to release or cleanse from your life. For example: *"I release stress and invite peace into my being."* Fold the paper and place it under the bowl of water to symbolize your intention grounding into the ritual.
5. **Reflect and Visualize** Look into the reflective water and see your face mirrored back at you. Imagine the water holding your intentions and washing away any negative energy. If using a mirror, gaze into it and let your thoughts flow, acknowledging what

you wish to release. Say: *"Water so deep, water so wide,*
Take from me what I no longer hide.
Reflect, renew, restore my soul,
Make me cleansed, make me whole."

6. **Anoint and Cleanse** Dip your fingers into the water and anoint your forehead, temples, and heart. As you do, feel a gentle wave of energy washing over you, clearing your mind and spirit. Say: *"By water's touch, my burdens fade,*
Cleanse my spirit, let worries wade.
Renew my heart, refresh my mind,
Leave the past, and peace I find."

7. **Complete the Purification** Splash a bit of the water on your hands or face, allowing the cool touch to invigorate you. If desired, use a soft cloth or towel to pat yourself dry, visualizing any last remnants of negativity being absorbed and released.

8. **Close the Ritual** Extinguish the candle and say: *"Thank you, water, crystal, and light,*
For cleansing me on this sacred night.
Renewed I stand, clear and free,
Grateful for the gift you've given me."

Carefully remove the crystals from the water and let them dry naturally. Dispose of the herbs respectfully, either by placing them in a compost or returning them to the earth.

Post-Ritual Practices

- **Maintain the Energy:** Carry one of the crystals (clear quartz, amethyst, or selenite) with you to maintain the cleansing energy.
- **Reflect in Your Journal:** Record your experience, any thoughts, or visions you had during the ritual. Writing helps solidify the release and renewal process.
- **Repeat as Needed:** This ritual can be performed whenever you feel the need to cleanse and rejuvenate your energy.

Enhancements for More Potency

- **Add a Moonlit Touch:** Leave the bowl of water out under the full moon overnight to enhance its energy before using it in the ritual.
- **Soothing Music:** Play soft, meditative music or nature sounds in the background to deepen your relaxation during the ritual.
- **Chanting or Mantras:** Repeat a simple mantra like *"I am cleansed, I am renewed"* throughout the ritual to reinforce your intention.

Practical Applications of the Spell

The *Crystal Pool Purification* spell is ideal for cleansing after stressful events, periods of illness, or emotional upheaval. It can also be used as a regular practice to maintain a balanced and clear energy field. This ritual supports emotional, mental, and spiritual health, ensuring that you remain grounded and refreshed as you navigate life's challenges.

By combining the fluid, reflective power of water with the steady, purifying energy of crystals, this ritual offers a profound means of self-care. Let the soothing embrace of the crystal pool cleanse you, restoring your inner harmony and illuminating your path forward.

Chapter 14: The Rain Dance Manifestation

A spell for manifesting intentions during or after rainfall

Introduction to the Spell

Rain has always been a powerful symbol of renewal, fertility, and cleansing across various cultures and traditions. Its rhythmic fall is said to wash away old energy, nurturing the earth and bringing new life. The *Rain Dance Manifestation* spell leverages this natural power to amplify your intentions, making it an ideal practice for manifesting desires when nature itself is charged with transformative energy. The spell draws upon the symbolism of rain as a bridge between the heavens and the earth, where wishes and intentions can be planted, nurtured, and brought to fruition.

This ritual can be performed during rainfall to harness its active energy or shortly after a rainstorm when the air is fresh and charged with potential. It is particularly effective for manifesting growth-related intentions, such as personal development, new projects, or opportunities.

The Symbolism of Rain in Magic

Rain represents purification, life-giving nourishment, and a bridge between the spiritual and earthly realms. The drops that fall from the sky carry the energy of the clouds and the atmosphere, creating a sacred connection between the heavens and the earth. This makes rain a powerful medium for carrying intentions and desires out into the universe. Dance, in many traditions, serves as an act of celebration, invocation, and connection to higher energies. Combining dance with rainfall brings a dynamic and joyful energy that enhances the power of manifestation.

Ideal Timing and Preparations

- **Best Time for the Ritual:** During rainfall or shortly after a rainstorm. The spell can also be performed on a day when rain is anticipated.
- **Moon Phase:** The new moon (for setting intentions) or the waxing moon (for growth and manifestation) are ideal.

- **Location:** Outdoors in a space where you can safely move under the rain or indoors near an open window where you can hear and feel the rain's energy.
- **Mindset:** Approach this ritual with an open heart, feeling gratitude for the rain and the opportunity it brings to align your energy with the flow of nature.

Materials Needed

- A small bowl or jar to collect rainwater (if outdoors)
- A piece of paper and a pen
- A green or blue candle (for growth and manifestation)
- A small stone or pebble (to ground your intention)
- Essential oil such as peppermint or eucalyptus (optional, for energizing the space)
- Comfortable clothing suitable for dancing
- Music with a rhythmic or nature-inspired beat (optional for enhancing the dance)

The Ritual: Step-by-Step Guide

1. **Prepare Your Space** Choose a spot outdoors where you can dance safely, or set up your space near an open window indoors. If collecting rainwater, place the bowl or jar in a location where it can fill with water. Place the candle in a sheltered spot where it will not be affected by the rain or breeze.
2. **Collect Rainwater (Optional)** If possible, collect a small amount of rainwater in the bowl or jar. This water will be charged with the energy of the storm and can be used for anointing or as a focus for your intention. Say: *"Rain of sky, pure and clear,*
Carry my wish, draw it near.
By each drop, intentions grow,
Manifest, let your power show."

3. **Ground and Center** Stand with your feet firmly planted on the ground. Close your eyes and take deep breaths, feeling the cool touch of the rain or the humid air around you. Visualize roots growing from your feet deep into the earth, anchoring you and connecting your energy to the steady heartbeat of the planet.
4. **Light the Candle** Light the green or blue candle and say: *"Candle bright, flame of might,*
Ignite my dreams, fuel my sight.
As rain falls, intentions rise,
Reach the stars, touch the skies."
5. **Write Your Intention** On the piece of paper, write down your specific intention or desire. Be clear and concise. For example: *"I manifest a new opportunity that aligns with my highest good."* Fold the paper and hold it close to your heart.
6. **Begin the Dance** Stand with your arms outstretched and feel the rain (or the presence of rain if indoors) as it touches your skin. Begin moving your body in a dance that feels natural and expressive. Let each movement symbolize the release of your intention, sending it up into the sky with the rhythm of the rain. If using music, let it guide your movements. Say: *"Dance with rain, dance with light,*
Carry my wish, day or night.
Flowing water, cleanse and bring,
The power of manifesting."
7. **Ground Your Intention** Hold the stone or pebble in your hand and press it against the paper with your written intention. Visualize your desire taking root like a seed planted in the rain-soaked earth, drawing nourishment from the elements. Say: *"Stone of earth, ground this spell,*
Let it grow and let it dwell.
With rain's touch, dreams take form,
Bring new life after the storm."

8. **Anoint Yourself with Rainwater (Optional)** Dip your fingers into the collected rainwater and anoint your forehead, temples, and heart, feeling the water's cool energy seep into your being. Say: *"Water of sky, essence divine,*
Let your power intertwine.
Wash me clean, renew my soul,
Bring forth abundance, full and whole."
9. **Conclude the Dance** Gradually slow your movements, coming to a gentle stop. Feel the rain or the air around you as a final blessing. Take a deep breath and let a sense of peace wash over you, knowing that your intention has been carried into the universe.
10. **Close the Ritual** Extinguish the candle safely and say: *"Thank you, rain, for your gift so sweet,*
For carrying my wish to meet.
By nature's power and nature's grace,
Manifestation takes its place."

Place the stone and paper in a special place or bury them in the ground as a symbolic act of planting your intention.

Post-Ritual Practices

- **Keep the Stone Close:** Carry the stone with you or place it on your altar as a reminder of the ritual and its ongoing energy.
- **Use the Rainwater:** If you collected rainwater, use it to anoint your pulse points before important meetings or moments when you need a boost of manifestation energy.
- **Reflect in Your Journal:** Write down your experience of the ritual, the emotions you felt, and any thoughts or ideas that came to you while dancing.

Enhancements for More Potency

- **Add Moonstone or Aquamarine:** Use these crystals during the ritual to enhance the water element's influence and support your intentions.
- **Chant or Affirmation:** Repeat an affirmation such as *"I am aligned with the flow of abundance"* throughout the day following the ritual.
- **Bathe in Rainwater:** If feasible, take a bath using the rainwater or infuse your bath with a few drops of it to continue the cleansing and manifesting process.

Practical Applications of the Spell

The *Rain Dance Manifestation* spell is perfect for initiating new projects, seeking positive change, or infusing your life with renewed energy and growth. It can be performed before starting a new job, moving to a new home, or entering a new phase of life. The ritual serves as a reminder that, like rain nourishing the earth, the universe can nourish and manifest your desires when intentions are clearly set and aligned with nature's energy.

By dancing with the rain and channeling its life-giving properties, you synchronize with the natural flow of the elements. Let this ritual be a celebration of your connection to nature and a powerful act of creation that sets your intentions into motion. Embrace the rain, dance with purpose, and watch your dreams take root and flourish.

Chapter 15: The Sunflower Guidance Ritual

A spell for finding direction and purpose, inspired by the path of sunflowers

Introduction to the Spell

Sunflowers are known for their unique ability to follow the sun, a phenomenon called heliotropism. This behavior symbolizes hope, direction, and the pursuit of light, embodying the essence of finding one's true path and purpose. The *Sunflower Guidance Ritual* draws inspiration from this natural phenomenon to help you find clarity, align with your goals, and understand the direction you should take. This spell channels the sunflower's energy to illuminate your path and provide insight into your life's purpose or current decisions.

Sunflowers, with their radiant blooms and unwavering focus on the sun, serve as a powerful metaphor for resilience, optimism, and the pursuit of clarity. By tapping into their symbolic energy, you can align yourself with these qualities and harness their guidance to light your way forward.

The Symbolism of Sunflowers in Magic

Sunflowers have long been associated with positivity, warmth, and spiritual growth. Their tall, sturdy stems and bright petals that reach for the sky embody the quest for personal growth and alignment with one's inner truth. In magical practice, sunflowers symbolize the sun's energy and are connected to the fire element, making them powerful conduits for spells centered around clarity, purpose, and direction.

Ideal Timing and Preparations

- **Best Time for the Ritual:** This ritual is most effective during the day, particularly at sunrise or late afternoon when the sun is prominent. It can also be performed during the waxing moon, which supports growth and manifestation.

- **Location:** An outdoor space surrounded by sunflowers or an indoor space with a sunflower plant or sunflower images.
- **Mindset:** Approach this ritual with openness and a willingness to seek answers. Be prepared to reflect on your current path and be receptive to guidance.

Materials Needed

- Fresh or dried sunflower petals (for embodying the sunflower's energy)
- A gold or yellow candle (representing the sun's light and clarity)
- A piece of citrine or sunstone (for amplifying purpose and confidence)
- A small bowl of sunflower seeds (symbolizing potential and growth)
- A piece of paper and a pen
- A mirror (optional, for self-reflection)
- Essential oil such as lemon or bergamot (to invoke a sense of focus and joy)

The Ritual: Step-by-Step Guide

1. **Set Up Your Sacred Space** Choose a space where you can be undisturbed, ideally near a window with sunlight streaming in or outdoors. Arrange the sunflower petals around the gold or yellow candle and place the citrine or sunstone next to it. Have the bowl of sunflower seeds and essential oil within reach.
2. **Anoint the Candle** Anoint the candle with a few drops of lemon or bergamot essential oil to infuse it with uplifting energy. As you do, say: *"Candle of gold, flame so bright,*
Guide my way, grant me sight.
With sunflower's strength and sun's embrace,
Show me my path, reveal my place."

3. **Light the Candle** Light the candle and take a moment to feel its warmth and radiance. Close your eyes and visualize yourself standing in a vast sunflower field, surrounded by tall blooms that all face the sun. Imagine their energy enveloping you, offering guidance and support.
4. **Ground and Center** Stand or sit with your feet on the ground. Take several deep breaths, feeling your body rooted to the earth. With each inhale, draw in the sun's energy; with each exhale, release any doubts or confusion clouding your mind.
5. **Reflect with the Sunflower Petals** Hold the sunflower petals in your hands and gently rub them between your fingers, feeling their texture and absorbing their energy. Say: *"Petals of light, petals of gold,*
Share the wisdom that you hold.
Just as you follow the sun so true,
Guide my steps, show me what to pursue."
6. **Set Your Intention** On the piece of paper, write a question or statement related to the guidance you seek. For example: *"What is my true purpose?"* or *"Which path should I take to achieve my goal?"* Hold the paper over your heart and close your eyes, visualizing your question being sent out to the universe with the candle's flame.
7. **Empower with the Crystal** Hold the citrine or sunstone in your dominant hand and visualize it glowing with a warm, golden light. Feel the energy of the crystal merging with your own, filling you with clarity and purpose. Say: *"Crystal of the sun, bring me light,*
Show me the way, clear and bright.
With each ray, dispel the dark,
Illuminate my journey, spark by spark."
8. **Eat the Sunflower Seeds (Optional)** If desired, eat a few sunflower seeds as a symbolic act of internalizing the guidance and energy of the sunflower. As you do, think of the seeds as tiny ves-

sels of potential that grow within you, helping you move forward with confidence.

9. **Gaze into the Mirror (Optional)** Hold the mirror so that it reflects the candle's light onto your face. This step enhances self-reflection and helps you see yourself clearly. Say: *"Mirror of truth, reflect my soul,*
Show me the path that makes me whole.
With clarity gained, I will find,
The purpose that aligns my mind."

10. **Close the Ritual** Extinguish the candle with gratitude, saying: *"Thank you, sun, thank you, bloom,*
For dispelling the fog and clearing the gloom.
My path is lit, my purpose found,
With guidance sure, I am earthbound."

Place the paper with your written intention in a safe space where you can revisit it. Keep the citrine or sunstone with you as a reminder of the guidance you received.

Post-Ritual Practices

- **Keep the Crystal Close:** Carry the citrine or sunstone with you, especially when making decisions or working toward your goals.
- **Journal Your Insights:** After the ritual, write down any thoughts, feelings, or images that came to you. This practice can help solidify the guidance received.
- **Nurture Sunflowers:** Plant sunflower seeds or care for a sunflower plant to maintain your connection to the energy of the ritual.

Enhancements for More Potency

- **Add Solar Incantations:** Chant or hum softly as you perform the ritual to invoke the sun's energy.

- **Visualize a Sun Path:** During meditation, imagine a path lit by the sun stretching out before you, guiding you toward your goal.
- **Morning Practice:** Repeat this ritual or aspects of it in the morning to strengthen your connection with the sun's energy and renew your sense of direction each day.

Practical Applications of the Spell

The *Sunflower Guidance Ritual* is perfect for times when you feel lost, are at a crossroads, or need clarity in your life's path. It can be performed before making major decisions, starting new projects, or when seeking inspiration for personal growth. The ritual encourages self-reflection and aligns you with the guiding energy of the sun and the sunflower, fostering a sense of purpose and confidence.

By tapping into the sunflower's natural inclination to seek the light, you create an energetic pathway that draws clarity and direction into your life. Let this ritual be your compass, guiding you through moments of uncertainty and helping you stay aligned with your highest purpose.

Chapter 16: Star-Woven Protection Spell
A nighttime ritual to guard against negativity and dark energy

Introduction to the Spell

The night sky, with its countless stars and cosmic expanse, has long symbolized the mystery of the universe and the protective energy of celestial light. The *Star-Woven Protection Spell* is a nighttime ritual designed to create a shield of star-like energy around you, guarding against negativity and dark influences. This spell weaves the protective and radiant energy of starlight into a personal barrier that surrounds you, bringing peace, safety, and a sense of cosmic connection.

This ritual is particularly effective during times of heightened stress, emotional vulnerability, or when facing negative environments or individuals. By invoking the light of the stars, you align yourself with the infinite power and purity of the cosmos, creating a protective aura that deflects negativity and fortifies your spirit.

The Symbolism of Stars in Magic

Stars have long represented hope, guidance, and protection in many cultures. They are seen as beacons of light in the darkness, embodying divine energy and the power of the universe. The act of weaving starlight into a protective barrier symbolizes drawing down cosmic energy to shield oneself from harm. This spell utilizes the celestial energy of stars to create an unyielding shield, invoking their light to dispel darkness and negative influences.

Ideal Timing and Preparations

- **Best Time for the Ritual:** This ritual is best performed on a clear night when the stars are visible. It is particularly powerful during a new moon for deep protection or a full moon to amplify the spell's energy.
- **Location:** An outdoor space where you can see the stars, such as a backyard or a balcony, is ideal. If this is not possible, an indoor space with a view of the night sky or an open window can work.

- **Mindset:** Approach this ritual with a sense of awe and connection to the vast universe. Feel open to receiving the light and protection of the stars.

Materials Needed

- A deep blue or black candle (representing the night sky)
- A small bowl of water (to reflect starlight)
- Star-shaped or moonstone crystals (for celestial energy)
- A silver or white cloth or scarf (symbolizing the fabric of starlight)
- Dried sage or rosemary (for protection)
- A piece of paper and a pen
- Essential oil such as frankincense or lavender (for calming and centering)
- A star charm or pendant (optional, to carry the protection with you)

The Ritual: Step-by-Step Guide

1. **Prepare Your Sacred Space** Choose a space where you can comfortably perform the ritual under the stars. Place the deep blue or black candle in the center and arrange the bowl of water, star-shaped or moonstone crystals, and dried herbs around it. Lay the silver or white cloth nearby.
2. **Cleanse the Space** Light the dried sage or rosemary and let the smoke waft around your space to cleanse it. As you do, say:
   "Herbs of earth, herbs of might,
   Clear this space, guard this night.
   Let no harm, let no fear,
   Enter now, come near."

Visualize the smoke carrying away any lingering negativity, leaving your space pure and protected.

1. **Ground and Center** Stand with your feet planted firmly on the ground. Close your eyes and take deep, steady breaths. Visualize roots extending from your feet into the earth, anchoring you. Feel the cool night air and the presence of the stars above as a calming force.
2. **Light the Candle** Light the deep blue or black candle and say:
"*Candle of night, dark yet bright,*
Burn with the strength of starlight.
Guard my soul, guard my space,
With cosmic power, fill this place."
3. **Reflect the Starlight** Hold the bowl of water up to the sky so that it reflects the stars. If indoors, hold the bowl close to a window where you can see the stars or imagine their presence. Say:
"*Water of night, mirror of sky,*
Reflect the stars, let protection lie.
By their light, woven tight,
Shield me now with cosmic might."
4. **Empower with Crystals** Place the star-shaped or moonstone crystals into the bowl of water. Visualize them absorbing the starlight and radiating a protective energy. Say: "*Crystals of stardust, pure and bright,*
Weave a shield, guard my sight.
Let this light, strong and true,
Defend and protect all I pursue."
5. **Set Your Protective Intention** On the piece of paper, write down your intention for protection. For example: "*May this star-woven shield protect me from negativity and dark energy, ensuring peace and safety.*" Fold the paper and place it under the candle.
6. **Wrap Yourself in Starlight** Take the silver or white cloth or scarf and hold it up to the sky. Visualize it being imbued with the light of the stars, becoming a fabric of protection. Drape it over your shoulders or around your body and say: "*Cloth of silver, woven bright,*

*Guard me well through darkest night.
Let no shadow, let no fear,
Break this shield, come near."*

7. **Create a Protective Aura** Close your eyes and visualize the stars above forming a shimmering, protective dome around you. Imagine this dome extending from your head to your feet, wrapping you in light that deflects any negative energy or harmful intentions. Say: *"Star of the sky, so divine,
Guard my heart, guard my mind.
Cosmic light, shining clear,
Protect me now, hold me near."*

8. **Conclude the Ritual** Gently touch the water with your fingers and anoint your forehead, temples, and heart. Say: *"By the starlight and by the flame,
I am protected, safe in name.
Shield of night, woven strong,
Guard me now, all night long."*

Extinguish the candle with gratitude and leave the bowl of water out overnight to continue absorbing the starlight. Dispose of the water in the morning by pouring it outside to return it to nature.

Post-Ritual Practices

- **Wear or Carry the Star Charm:** If you have a star pendant or charm, wear it as a reminder of your protective shield and to carry the energy of the ritual with you.
- **Visualize the Shield Daily:** Each night before sleeping, visualize the star-woven shield surrounding you, reinforcing its power.
- **Place Crystals Nearby:** Keep the moonstone or star-shaped crystals near your bed or workspace to maintain a sense of protection.

Enhancements for More Potency

- **Add Celestial Music:** Play soft, ethereal music that evokes the feeling of the night sky to enhance the atmosphere during the ritual.
- **Chant a Protective Mantra:** Repeat a mantra such as *"I am guarded by the stars' embrace"* during meditation to strengthen the spell's effects.
- **Moonlight Infusion:** Leave the cloth or scarf out under the full moon overnight before using it in the ritual to enhance its protective energy.

Practical Applications of the Spell

The *Star-Woven Protection Spell* is especially useful during times of stress, before entering difficult situations, or when you feel particularly vulnerable to negative energy. It can be performed whenever you need to create a sense of safety and peace, whether for yourself or for loved ones. This spell connects you to the vast, unwavering energy of the cosmos, providing comfort and a shield that extends beyond the physical.

By drawing on the light of the stars and the boundless power of the night sky, you weave a protective barrier that guards against darkness and negativity. Let this ritual be your cosmic safeguard, surrounding you with the strength and light of the universe, ready to face whatever comes your way.

Chapter 17: The Evergreen Wealth Spell
A nature-inspired spell to draw abundance and financial stability

Introduction to the Spell

Throughout history, nature has been a powerful symbol of abundance and continuous growth. Evergreen trees, in particular, represent resilience, prosperity, and everlasting life due to their ability to remain lush and vibrant even in the harshest conditions. The *Evergreen Wealth Spell* channels the energy of these steadfast trees to attract financial stability, growth, and sustained abundance. This nature-inspired ritual combines elements associated with prosperity, tapping into the timeless strength and vitality of the evergreen to draw wealth and stability into your life.

This spell can be used when seeking new financial opportunities, growing an existing income stream, or enhancing overall financial security. By connecting with the evergreen's essence, you align yourself with a source of energy that embodies unyielding growth and continuous renewal.

The Symbolism of Evergreens in Magic

Evergreens, such as pine, cedar, and fir, are known for their persistent greenness and their ability to thrive year-round. They symbolize longevity, protection, and wealth due to their natural resilience. In magical practice, evergreens are associated with stability, growth, and prosperity, making them ideal elements for spells aimed at financial success and sustainability.

Ideal Timing and Preparations

- **Best Time for the Ritual:** This spell is most effective during the waxing moon (for growth) or on a Thursday, which is ruled by Jupiter, the planet of abundance and expansion.
- **Location:** A quiet space surrounded by nature, such as a forest or garden, is ideal. If outdoors is not possible, an indoor space with potted plants or nature-themed decorations works well.
- **Mindset:** Approach this ritual with gratitude for the abundance that already exists in your life and an open heart ready to receive more.

Materials Needed

- A green or gold candle (for wealth and growth)
- Fresh evergreen branches or leaves (such as pine or cedar)
- A small bowl of earth or potting soil
- Cinnamon sticks or ground cinnamon (to boost prosperity)
- A piece of jade or green aventurine (for financial growth)
- A piece of paper and a pen
- Essential oil such as pine or patchouli (for invoking nature's essence)
- A small coin or token symbolizing wealth

The Ritual: Step-by-Step Guide

1. **Set Up Your Sacred Space** Find a space where you feel connected to nature, whether outdoors or in a room adorned with natural elements. Place the green or gold candle in the center, surrounded by the evergreen branches and bowl of earth. Arrange the cinnamon, jade or green aventurine, and coin nearby.
2. **Anoint the Candle** Anoint the candle with pine or patchouli essential oil, focusing on your intention of drawing abundance into your life. As you anoint it, say: *"Candle of green, flame of gold,*
Draw wealth and abundance, manifold.
With evergreen's spirit, strong and bright,
Bring prosperity into my sight."
3. **Light the Candle** Light the candle and let its flame represent the spark of new financial opportunities. Close your eyes for a moment and feel its warmth infuse the space with energy. Say: *"Flame of fortune, flame so true,*
Ignite abundance, renew, renew.
By this light, my wealth shall grow,
Like evergreen, steady and slow."
4. **Ground with the Earth** Hold the bowl of earth in your hands and feel its weight. Visualize the rich, fertile soil nurturing seeds that grow into strong, evergreen trees. Place the bowl in front of the candle and say: *"Earth below, rich and deep,*
Hold my fortune, let it keep.
Like the forest, endless and strong,
Prosperity comes, steady and long."
5. **Create the Evergreen Bundle** Take the evergreen branches or leaves and bind them with the cinnamon sticks using a piece of twine or simply hold them together. The evergreens symbolize resilience and wealth, while the cinnamon adds an element of

swift luck and prosperity. Hold the bundle and say: *"Evergreens of green, leaves of might,*
Guard my wealth, day and night.
Cinnamon's fire, warm and swift,
Bring abundance, bring the gift."

6. **Set Your Intention** On the piece of paper, write a clear statement of your intention. For example: *"I attract financial stability and continuous growth in my career/business."* Fold the paper and place it under the bowl of earth to root your intention in the foundation of nature.

7. **Empower with the Crystal** Hold the jade or green aventurine in your dominant hand and visualize it glowing with a soft, green light. Imagine this light radiating from the crystal and merging with the candle flame, creating a flow of energy that attracts wealth and abundance. Say: *"Crystal of growth, stone of gain,*
Draw prosperity without strain.
Let wealth flow, steady and sure,
With evergreen's power, rich and pure."

8. **Add the Coin** Place the coin on top of the folded paper beneath the bowl of earth. This symbolizes the tangible aspect of wealth and serves as a token that binds your intention to reality. Say: *"Token of wealth, metal bright,*
Anchor my wishes, hold them tight.
Let abundance rise and stay,
Growing more with each new day."

9. **Envision the Path of Prosperity** Spend a few moments in quiet meditation, visualizing a lush forest of evergreens growing around you. Imagine these trees representing your financial journey—strong, steady, and ever-expanding. Feel the energy of prosperity flowing through you, rooted and unyielding.

10. **Close the Ritual** Extinguish the candle with gratitude, saying: *"Thank you, earth, and thank you, flame,*
For this gift in fortune's name.

Evergreen, ever bright,
Guard my wealth, day and night."

Leave the evergreen bundle near your workspace or altar as a reminder of the spell. Keep the crystal close, either in your pocket or in a place where you handle it often, to maintain the spell's energy.

Post-Ritual Practices

- **Keep the Crystal with You:** Carry the jade or green aventurine with you as a talisman for ongoing financial growth.
- **Reflect in a Journal:** Write down any insights or ideas that come to you in the days following the ritual, as this can guide you toward new opportunities.
- **Reinforce the Spell Weekly:** Hold the evergreen bundle and repeat your intention once a week to keep the energy strong.

Enhancements for More Potency

- **Create an Evergreen Sachet:** Place some evergreen leaves and cinnamon sticks in a small cloth pouch to carry with you as a charm for attracting wealth.
- **Incorporate Green Incense:** Burn incense such as sandalwood or frankincense during the ritual to deepen the atmosphere of abundance.
- **Repeat with the New Moon:** Perform this ritual every new moon to reinforce the energy of growth and renewal.

Practical Applications of the Spell

The *Evergreen Wealth Spell* is perfect for times when you seek financial stability, growth in your business or career, or want to manifest an influx of wealth into your life. It can be performed before starting new ventures, making significant financial decisions, or when you feel the need to reinforce your financial foundation.

By tapping into the steadfast energy of evergreens and the nurturing power of the earth, this ritual helps you build a strong and continuous flow of prosperity. Let the unyielding spirit of the evergreen guide you, ensuring that your financial journey remains steady and fruitful. Embrace this natural energy as a reminder that true abundance, like nature, is deeply rooted, continuously growing, and unwavering.

Chapter 18: The Echoing Grove Spell for Connection

A spell to strengthen bonds with loved ones, near or far

Introduction to the Spell

In our fast-paced world, maintaining strong and meaningful connections with those we hold dear can be challenging. The *Echoing Grove Spell for Connection* is designed to foster and strengthen bonds with loved ones, whether they are close by or far away. This nature-inspired ritual taps into the energy of the forest grove, a place where trees communicate silently through their roots and where nature's interconnectedness is palpable. By channeling the essence of a grove's unity, this spell enhances empathy, understanding, and emotional closeness, nurturing the bonds you share with family and friends.

The ritual is especially effective during times of physical distance or emotional strain. It can be performed when you want to reinforce existing relationships, reach out energetically to those far away, or heal rifts that have developed over time.

The Symbolism of the Grove in Magic

Grove magic symbolizes community, unity, and the deep bonds that tie beings together. In nature, groves of trees share resources and communicate through root systems, embodying the idea of interconnection and mutual support. This spell channels the quiet wisdom and networked strength of the grove to weave stronger, deeper ties between you and those you love.

Ideal Timing and Preparations

- **Best Time for the Ritual:** This spell is best performed during the waxing moon (for growth and strengthening) or the full

moon (for amplifying connection). Early evening or dawn are ideal times to connect with nature's energy.
- **Location:** An outdoor space surrounded by trees or plants is perfect, but an indoor space decorated with greenery or images of a forest can also work.
- **Mindset:** Approach the ritual with a sense of love, gratitude, and openness. Visualize the faces of those you want to connect with and focus on positive emotions.

Materials Needed

- A circle of twine or green ribbon (symbolizing unity and connection)
- Fresh or dried leaves (such as oak, maple, or ivy for strength and bonding)
- A small bowl of saltwater (for cleansing and emotional balance)
- A piece of rose quartz or amethyst (to enhance love and understanding)
- A green or pink candle (for harmony and love)
- A small piece of paper and a pen
- Essential oil such as cedarwood or rose (to invoke a sense of warmth and connection)
- A sprig of lavender or rosemary (optional, for peace and clarity)

The Ritual: Step-by-Step Guide

1. **Prepare Your Sacred Space** Arrange your space to create a circle of connection. Place the green or pink candle in the center, surrounded by the leaves, bowl of saltwater, rose quartz or amethyst, and twine or ribbon. If using essential oil, anoint the candle with a few drops before starting.
2. **Cleanse the Space** Sprinkle a few drops of the saltwater around your ritual space to purify it and prepare for positive, loving en-

ergy. As you do, say: *"Salt of sea, water clear,*
Cleanse this space, draw loved ones near.
Let our bonds, steady and true,
Be strengthened now, renewed anew."

3. **Ground and Center** Stand or sit comfortably with your feet planted on the ground. Close your eyes, breathe deeply, and visualize roots growing from your feet into the earth. Feel the energy of the grove surrounding you, connecting you to a vast network of supportive and loving energy.

4. **Light the Candle** Light the green or pink candle and say: *"Candle of harmony, candle of light,*
Bring warmth and connection through day and night.
Flame that glows, bond that grows,
Link my heart where love flows."

5. **Invoke the Energy of the Grove** Hold the leaves in your hands and envision the forest grove, where each tree stands strong yet connected to others through an unseen network. Feel the leaves' energy and imagine it spreading warmth and love through your bonds. Say: *"Leaves of green, strong and wise,*
Echoing whispers, heartfelt ties.
Unite us now, near and far,
Connect us strong, like root to star."

6. **Set Your Intention** On the piece of paper, write the names of the loved ones you wish to strengthen your connection with. Add a simple affirmation, such as *"Our bond is unbreakable, supported by love and understanding."* Fold the paper and hold it close to your heart, feeling the warmth of the candle's flame and the energy of the grove surrounding you.

7. **Bind with Twine or Ribbon** Take the twine or ribbon and gently wrap it around the leaves and paper, tying a simple knot at the end. This represents the unity and strength of your connections. Say: *"Twine of green, hold and weave,*
Strengthen the bonds that I believe.

With each knot, love and light,
Guard our hearts, through dark and bright."

8. **Empower with the Crystal** Place the rose quartz or amethyst on top of the tied bundle. Visualize a soft pink or purple glow emanating from the crystal, spreading to everyone whose name you wrote. Say: *"Crystal of love, crystal of grace,*
Fill our hearts, fill this space.
Let empathy flow, understanding bloom,
Dispel all distance, clear all gloom."

9. **Anoint with Essential Oil (Optional)** Dab a bit of cedarwood or rose oil on your wrists or the tied bundle to deepen the ritual's energy. As you do, repeat: *"Scent of love, warm and sweet,*
Bring closeness where hearts meet.
Strengthen ties, make them last,
Keep our bond, future and past."

10. **Complete the Ritual** Gently touch the bowl of saltwater and sprinkle a few drops over the tied bundle, sealing the spell. Extinguish the candle with gratitude and say: *"Thank you, grove, thank you, light,*
For bringing hearts together tonight.
Our bonds are strong, woven deep,
Connected always, in wake and sleep."

Place the tied bundle and crystal in a safe space where you can see them as a reminder of the connection. Keep the candle to use again for future rituals or moments when you wish to reconnect.

Post-Ritual Practices

- **Keep the Crystal Nearby:** Carry the rose quartz or amethyst with you to maintain the energy of connection and love.
- **Check In with Loved Ones:** Reach out to the people you included in your ritual and spend time communicating with them. This action reinforces the energy of the spell.

- **Repeat as Needed:** Perform this ritual whenever you feel distant from loved ones or want to strengthen your emotional bonds.

Enhancements for More Potency

- **Create a Grove Talisman:** Place some of the dried leaves and a small piece of the tied twine into a small pouch to carry as a charm for connection.
- **Add Music:** Play gentle, forest-inspired music or nature sounds to evoke the feeling of being in a grove during the ritual.
- **Visualization Practice:** Spend a few minutes each day visualizing the people you love surrounded by a warm, golden light, strengthening your shared connection.

Practical Applications of the Spell

The *Echoing Grove Spell for Connection* is especially beneficial during times when distance, stress, or life changes have impacted your relationships. It can be performed before reconnecting with old friends, when seeking to heal a strained relationship, or simply as a way to remind your loved ones that they are cherished and supported.

By drawing on the interconnected strength of a grove, this spell encourages deeper understanding and empathy, fostering unity and warmth. Let this ritual serve as a reminder that, like the trees of a grove, we are all connected by unseen roots of love and support. Embrace the enduring power of the forest and let it echo through your bonds, bringing closeness and harmony to those you hold dear.

Chapter 19: The Mist's Disappearance Spell
A ritual for letting go of past burdens or negative influences

Introduction to the Spell

Carrying past burdens or lingering negative influences can feel like a fog clouding your mind and spirit. The *Mist's Disappearance Spell* is designed to help you release these heavy energies and find clarity and renewal. Inspired by the gentle, ephemeral nature of mist, which dissipates as the sun rises, this ritual symbolizes the process of letting go and allowing emotional and energetic release. The mist embodies the idea of transient states; it is present for a moment, and then it vanishes, leaving behind fresh, clear air.

This spell can be particularly powerful during times of transition, emotional healing, or when you need to break free from repetitive patterns or thoughts that no longer serve you. By invoking the cleansing and vanishing properties of mist, you can let go of past burdens and step into a more harmonious state of being.

The Symbolism of Mist in Magic

Mist represents the in-between, the transition from one state to another. It is associated with the element of water and holds qualities of purification, obscurity, and release. In magical practices, mist is used as a metaphor for the process of letting go—what once was solid becomes light, transparent, and eventually fades away. This ritual harnesses the essence of mist to dissolve emotional heaviness, banish negative influences, and clear the way for renewal.

Ideal Timing and Preparations

- **Best Time for the Ritual:** Early morning as the mist naturally forms or during the waning moon, which is ideal for banishing and releasing.

- **Location:** An outdoor space where mist or dew can be felt or observed is ideal. If outdoors isn't possible, an indoor space where you can create a mist (such as with a spray bottle of water) can be used.
- **Mindset:** Approach this ritual with a readiness to release and a willingness to move forward. Be gentle with yourself and set the intention to embrace clarity and peace.

Materials Needed

- A light blue or white candle (for purification and clarity)
- A small bowl of water (to represent the essence of mist)
- Dried sage or eucalyptus (for cleansing)
- A small mirror (to reflect and release the past)
- A piece of paper and a pen
- A drop of essential oil such as lavender or peppermint (optional, for calming and clearing energy)
- A feather or fan (to symbolize the dispersal of mist)
- A soft cloth or scarf (optional, to symbolize letting go)

The Ritual: Step-by-Step Guide

1. **Prepare Your Sacred Space** Choose a quiet space where you can be undisturbed. Place the light blue or white candle at the center and surround it with the bowl of water, the mirror, and dried sage or eucalyptus. Keep the piece of paper, pen, feather or fan, and cloth within easy reach.
2. **Cleanse the Space** Light the dried sage or eucalyptus and waft the smoke around your ritual space to clear any residual negative energy. As you cleanse, say: *"Smoke of sage, pure and light,*
Cleanse this space, day or night.
Let the past fade, let burdens cease,
Bring this place a sense of peace."

3. **Ground and Center** Sit comfortably and close your eyes. Take deep, steady breaths, feeling yourself connected to the ground beneath you. Visualize a gentle mist surrounding you, holding your burdens and negative influences. Imagine that this mist is ready to dissipate with your intention.

4. **Light the Candle** Light the candle and say: *"Candle of clarity, candle of might,*
Illuminate shadows, dissolve the night.
With this flame, I let it go,
Burdens lift, light will flow."

5. **Set Your Intention** On the piece of paper, write down what you wish to release. This could be past regrets, fears, negative self-talk, or influences that no longer serve you. Fold the paper and hold it in your hands, visualizing the burdens trapped within its fibers. Say: *"Words on paper, weight of heart,*
I release you now, we part.
Into the mist, you shall fade,
And a clearer path will be made."

6. **Invoke the Energy of Mist** Hold the bowl of water up to the candle and imagine it turning into mist, ready to carry away your burdens. If indoors, you can lightly spray water into the air with a spray bottle to create the sensation of mist. Say: *"Mist so light, mist so free,*
Take what's heavy, take what's me.
Dissolve the past, let it rise,
Disperse in air, touch the skies."

7. **Reflect with the Mirror** Take the small mirror and gaze into it, imagining that it reflects the burdens you hold. See these burdens dissolve into mist within the reflection, becoming lighter and lighter until they disappear. Say: *"Mirror of reflection, show me release,*
Transform my burden, bring me peace.

Fade into air, let go, let be,
What once held me, now sets me free."

8. **Use the Feather or Fan** Use the feather or fan to gently waft air around you, symbolizing the dispersal of the mist and the burdens it holds. Visualize the mist lifting and the air around you becoming clear. Say: *"Feather's breath, gentle and light,*
Carry away shadows of night.
Let the mist rise, let it part,
Bring me clarity, heal my heart."

9. **Release with the Water** Dip your fingers in the bowl of water and touch your temples and heart, symbolizing the final act of release. Say: *"With this water, I cleanse and clear,*
Past dissolves, no more to fear.
Purified, renewed, I stand,
Released from burdens, heart in hand."

10. **Conclude the Ritual** Gently touch the paper to the candle flame and let it burn in a safe dish (optional). As it turns to ash, say: *"Thank you, mist, thank you, light,*
For taking burdens into flight.
I am free, I am whole,
With clarity restored, I reach my goal."

Extinguish the candle with gratitude and place the mirror and feather aside as a reminder of your newfound clarity.

Post-Ritual Practices

- **Keep the Mirror Nearby:** Place the mirror in your room or workspace as a reminder of your release and to reflect back any new clarity you gain.
- **Visualize Daily:** Spend a few moments each day visualizing the mist carrying away any small worries or burdens, reinforcing the spell's energy.

- **Repeat if Necessary:** This ritual can be repeated whenever you feel weighed down by past events or negative influences.

Enhancements for More Potency

- **Add Music:** Play soft, calming music or nature sounds to evoke the atmosphere of a misty morning and deepen your relaxation.
- **Use a Cloth or Scarf:** Hold a soft cloth and let it fall gently to the ground at the end of the ritual to symbolize the final act of letting go.
- **Create a Mist Infusion:** Infuse the water with a few drops of lavender or peppermint essential oil before the ritual for added calming and clearing effects.

Practical Applications of the Spell

The *Mist's Disappearance Spell* is ideal for anyone experiencing emotional burdens, past regrets, or ongoing negative influences. It can be used as part of a regular self-care routine or during significant life transitions when letting go is crucial for personal growth. This spell encourages emotional release and mental clarity, empowering you to move forward unencumbered by what once weighed you down.

By harnessing the ethereal energy of mist, you create a process that mirrors the natural cycles of release and renewal. This ritual allows you to transform emotional heaviness into lightness, reminding you that what may seem overwhelming at first can become something that dissipates, leaving you with a clearer mind and a freer spirit. Embrace the disappearing mist as a sign that you are ready to let go and step into the clarity that awaits you.

Chapter 20: The Sage Wisdom Incantation

A spell to access deeper wisdom and insight using sage

Introduction to the Spell

Sage has been revered for centuries in cultures across the world for its cleansing, protective, and wisdom-enhancing properties. Known for its ability to purify spaces and energy, sage is also believed to open pathways to higher knowledge and deeper understanding. The *Sage Wisdom Incantation* is a ritual designed to help you access your inner wisdom and connect with the profound insights that lie within and beyond your conscious mind. By engaging with sage's potent energy, you can deepen your intuition, unlock hidden knowledge, and gain clarity on complex situations.

This spell is perfect for moments when you need guidance, seek answers to significant questions, or wish to enhance your overall spiritual awareness. By invoking the properties of sage, this ritual allows you to tune into your higher self and the wisdom of the universe.

The Symbolism of Sage in Magic

Sage is known for its dual role as a cleanser and an enhancer of spiritual awareness. In many traditions, it is burned to clear negative energy and create a sacred space for meditation, reflection, and ritual work. Sage's smoke is believed to carry prayers, thoughts, and intentions to the spiritual realm, making it an excellent tool for deepening one's connection to wisdom and insight. This spell uses sage to open pathways to knowledge and create a receptive state for profound understanding.

Ideal Timing and Preparations

- **Best Time for the Ritual:** The full moon or a Thursday, a day associated with Jupiter, which symbolizes wisdom, learning, and expansion. Dusk is an ideal time for this ritual when day transi-

tions into night, symbolizing the move from conscious thought to deeper understanding.
- **Location:** A quiet, sacred space where you can focus without interruptions. It can be indoors with a clear view of the moon or surrounded by items that promote introspection.
- **Mindset:** Approach this ritual with an open mind and a willingness to receive insights. Be prepared to listen and be guided by the wisdom that emerges.

Materials Needed

- A bundle of dried sage or loose sage leaves
- A fire-safe dish or abalone shell (for burning sage)
- A white or purple candle (for clarity and spiritual insight)
- A small piece of paper and a pen
- Amethyst or clear quartz crystal (to enhance intuition)
- A small bowl of water (to symbolize receptivity)
- Essential oil such as sage or frankincense (optional, for deepening the ritual)
- A comfortable chair or meditation cushion

The Ritual: Step-by-Step Guide

1. **Prepare Your Sacred Space** Choose a quiet space and arrange your items. Place the white or purple candle in the center, surrounded by the bowl of water, amethyst or clear quartz crystal, and the fire-safe dish with sage. Anoint the candle with a drop of essential oil if desired, and place it in a safe holder.
2. **Cleanse the Space** Light the sage bundle or loose sage leaves and allow the smoke to fill your space. As the smoke rises, gently waft it with your hand or a feather around your body and throughout the area. Say: *"Sage of wisdom, herb of sight,*
Cleanse this space, draw in the light.

Clear the mind, open the way,
Bring deeper wisdom to this day."

3. **Ground and Center** Sit in a comfortable chair or on a cushion with your feet firmly on the ground. Close your eyes and take deep, steady breaths. Visualize roots growing from the base of your spine or feet into the earth, anchoring you and drawing in steady, nurturing energy. Feel yourself connected and centered.
4. **Light the Candle** Light the white or purple candle and say:
"Candle bright, flame of the wise,
Shine your light, open my eyes.
Illuminate shadows, guide my sight,
Bring wisdom now, pure and bright."

Allow the candle's flame to represent the spark of insight you seek.

1. **Focus with the Crystal** Hold the amethyst or clear quartz crystal in your dominant hand. Close your eyes and feel the energy of the crystal connecting with your own. Imagine it amplifying your intuition and clearing your mind of clutter. Say: *"Crystal of insight, clear and true,*
Amplify wisdom, help me view.
Deep within and far beyond,
Bring me answers, clear and fond."
2. **Set Your Intention** On the piece of paper, write down a question or intention related to the wisdom or insight you seek. For example: *"What should be my next step in my career?"* or *"Reveal the truth I need to understand about [situation]."* Fold the paper and place it under the bowl of water.
3. **Invoke the Energy of Sage** Hold the sage close to your face and take a deep breath, inhaling its earthy scent (without inhaling the smoke). Visualize the smoke carrying your question into the universe, where it will be met with guidance and insight. Say: *"Sage of earth, sage of sky,*

Lift my spirit, hear my cry.
Bring the answers, wise and old,
Let the truth and insights unfold."

4. **Connect with the Water** Dip your fingers into the bowl of water and touch your third eye (the space between your eyebrows) and your heart. Feel the coolness as a symbol of receptivity and openness to wisdom. Say: *"Water of life, water so still,*
Open my mind, bend to my will.
Let intuition flow, strong and clear,
Bring wisdom close, let it appear."

5. **Meditative State** Sit quietly and gaze at the candle flame. Let your mind clear and become receptive to any thoughts, images, or feelings that arise. You may feel the urge to close your eyes and enter a light meditative state. Trust whatever comes to you, even if it seems abstract at first. Spend at least 10-15 minutes in this reflective state.

6. **Close the Ritual** To conclude, thank the sage and the energies you have invoked. Extinguish the candle and say: *"Thank you, sage, thank you, light,*
For guiding me with wisdom tonight.
Clarity gained, insight found,
With gratitude, I am now unbound."

Allow the sage to burn out safely or snuff it out, preserving the remnants for future use.

Post-Ritual Practices

- **Reflect in Your Journal:** Write down any insights or images that came to you during the ritual. Even seemingly insignificant details can become meaningful over time.
- **Keep the Crystal Close:** Carry the amethyst or clear quartz with you or place it near your workspace to maintain a connection to the energy of wisdom.

- **Follow Up with Action:** If you received clear guidance or inspiration, take steps to act on it. Trust that the insights you gained will support your journey.

Enhancements for More Potency

- **Add Soft Music:** Play meditative or ambient music in the background to enhance your focus and deepen your relaxation.
- **Chant a Mantra:** Repeat a mantra such as *"Wisdom flows to me easily"* or *"I am open to universal knowledge"* during the meditation.
- **Moonlight Infusion:** Place the bowl of water under the moon overnight before the ritual to enhance its connection to intuition and insight.

Practical Applications of the Spell

The *Sage Wisdom Incantation* is ideal for moments when you need clarity on important decisions, seek spiritual insight, or wish to enhance your intuitive abilities. It can be used as part of a larger spiritual practice or as a standalone ritual when facing particularly challenging questions.

By invoking the energy of sage and incorporating symbolic elements such as the crystal and water, this spell helps you access wisdom that lies beyond the conscious mind. Trust in the process and allow yourself to be guided by the light of insight that sage and ritual magic can provide. Embrace the newfound clarity and take confident steps forward, knowing that the wisdom of the ages is at your side.

Chapter 21: River's Flow Creativity Booster

A spell for enhancing creative flow and inspiration

Introduction to the Spell

The flow of a river is a powerful metaphor for creativity. Just as a river courses steadily through landscapes, shaping its path and bringing life wherever it goes, creativity flows through the mind, shaping ideas and fueling inspiration. The *River's Flow Creativity Booster* spell is designed to tap into the dynamic energy of water to enhance your creative flow and awaken inspiration. This ritual channels the power of the river to break through creative blocks, encourage innovative thinking, and provide clarity for artistic or problem-solving endeavors.

Ideal for artists, writers, musicians, and anyone needing a boost in creativity, this spell uses elements that symbolize fluidity, adaptability, and inspiration. By connecting with the essence of a river's flow, you can tap into a boundless source of ideas and unlock your creative potential.

The Symbolism of Rivers in Magic

Rivers symbolize movement, change, adaptability, and renewal. They are associated with the water element, which governs emotions, intuition, and the subconscious mind—key components of the creative process. The continuous, unyielding flow of a river represents the ability to keep moving forward despite obstacles, making it an ideal symbol for overcoming creative blocks and revitalizing inspiration. This spell uses the river's qualities to invigorate and empower your creative energy.

Ideal Timing and Preparations

- **Best Time for the Ritual:** This spell is best performed during a waxing moon (to build energy and inspiration) or in the morning when the day is fresh and full of potential.
- **Location:** Near a body of flowing water, such as a river or stream, is ideal. If this isn't possible, an indoor space with a bowl of water can work, especially if accompanied by a recording of river sounds.

- **Mindset:** Approach this ritual with an open mind and a sense of curiosity. Be ready to let go of expectations and allow your creativity to flow freely.

Materials Needed

- A blue or light green candle (to symbolize water and inspiration)
- A small bowl of spring or filtered water (representing the river)
- Fresh or dried mint leaves (for mental clarity and stimulation)
- A piece of aquamarine or blue lace agate (to enhance communication and creative flow)
- A piece of paper and a pen
- Essential oil such as peppermint or eucalyptus (optional, for mental clarity)
- A small, flat stone or pebble (symbolizing grounded inspiration)

The Ritual: Step-by-Step Guide

1. **Set Up Your Sacred Space** Choose a quiet space and arrange your items. Place the blue or light green candle at the center, surrounded by the bowl of water, mint leaves, and crystal. Keep the piece of paper, pen, and pebble nearby. If using essential oil, anoint the candle with a drop for added clarity.
2. **Cleanse the Space** Before beginning, close your eyes and take a few deep breaths. Visualize a clear, flowing river washing through your space, carrying away stagnant energy and filling the area with freshness. Say: *"River pure, river bright,*
Cleanse this space, bring creative light.
Let energy flow, let inspiration rise,
Guide my spirit, clear my eyes."
3. **Light the Candle** Light the blue or light green candle and watch its flame dance like sunlight on water. Say: *"Candle of water, flame so true,*

Ignite my mind, renew, renew.
By river's flow and liquid grace,
Bring inspiration to this place."

4. **Invoke the Power of Water** Hold the bowl of water in your hands and gaze into its reflective surface. Imagine it as a miniature river, brimming with ideas and energy. Say: *"Water of life, fluid and free,*
Carry ideas and visions to me.
Flowing fast, flowing deep,
Wake my mind from its sleep."

5. **Add the Mint Leaves** Drop the fresh or dried mint leaves into the water, visualizing them infusing the water with their stimulating properties. Say: *"Mint of green, crisp and bright,*
Awaken thoughts, clear as light.
Let your essence, sharp and pure,
Stir creativity, make it sure."

6. **Hold the Crystal** Take the aquamarine or blue lace agate in your dominant hand and close your eyes. Feel its cool, calming energy spreading through your hand and up your arm, reaching your mind and opening pathways to creative thought. Say: *"Crystal of blue, inspire me now,*
Unlock the mind, show me how.
Bring forth visions, bring them near,
Make the path of creation clear."

7. **Write Your Intention** On the piece of paper, write down a brief statement such as *"I am open to the flow of inspiration and creative ideas."* Place the paper under the bowl of water and imagine your intention sinking into the water, carried by its currents.

8. **Connect with the Pebble** Hold the small, flat pebble in your hand and imagine it being shaped by the flowing water of the river. It represents your ability to stay grounded while letting ideas flow around and through you. Say: *"Pebble smooth, shaped by flow,*

*Let my ideas freely grow.
Ground my thoughts, steady and clear,
Let inspiration draw me near."*

9. **Immerse in the River's Energy** Dip your fingers into the bowl of water and touch your forehead, temples, and heart. Feel the cool water awakening your senses and connecting you to the energy of the river. Close your eyes and visualize yourself standing at the edge of a flowing river, feeling the breeze and hearing the rush of water. Say: *"River's touch, awaken my sight,
Fill me with wonder, fill me with light.
Ideas flow, boundless and true,
Creativity rise, I welcome you."*

10. **Conclude the Ritual** Gently touch the pebble to the candle's flame (be careful not to let it burn) as a symbolic act of merging fire and water—clarity and inspiration. Extinguish the candle with gratitude and say: *"Thank you, river, thank you, flame,
For bringing creative thoughts to claim.
May inspiration flow like a stream,
Awake and alive, within my dream."*

Keep the bowl of water near your workspace until the next morning, and then pour it outside onto the earth as an offering to nature.

Post-Ritual Practices

- **Keep the Crystal Close:** Carry the aquamarine or blue lace agate with you or place it on your desk to keep your creative energy flowing.
- **Reflect and Create:** Spend time journaling or engaging in a creative activity shortly after the ritual to harness the newfound energy.
- **Use the Pebble as a Talisman:** Keep the pebble on your workspace as a reminder that inspiration flows like a river when you stay open and grounded.

Enhancements for More Potency

- **Play River Sounds:** Play a recording of flowing water during the ritual to enhance the ambiance and deepen your connection to the river's energy.
- **Add Aromatherapy:** Diffuse peppermint or eucalyptus essential oil in your space to clear your mind and enhance mental clarity.
- **Chant a Creativity Mantra:** Repeat a mantra such as *"Creativity flows through me like a river"* while meditating to maintain the spell's energy.

Practical Applications of the Spell

The *River's Flow Creativity Booster* spell is perfect for anyone experiencing creative blocks, starting a new project, or seeking inspiration for ongoing work. It can be performed regularly as part of your creative routine or used when you need an extra push to reignite your inspiration. By connecting with the energy of the river, you learn to let go of resistance and allow your ideas to flow naturally and effortlessly.

Embrace the power of water and the adaptability of the river as a symbol of continuous creation and renewal. Let this spell be your guide to tapping into an endless stream of ideas, fueling your creativity, and helping you move through any creative challenges with ease and grace.

Chapter 22: The Firefly's Light of Truth
A night-time spell for uncovering hidden truths

Introduction to the Spell

The firefly, with its bioluminescent glow, has long been a symbol of illumination, hope, and the revelation of hidden truths. Their light dances across the night, showing brief yet brilliant flashes that guide and inspire. The *Firefly's Light of Truth* spell harnesses this gentle, illuminating energy to uncover hidden truths in your life, whether they pertain to personal clarity, uncovering secrets, or understanding a complex situation. This ritual is performed at night, under the cover of darkness when the light of truth is most needed and most powerful.

This spell can be used when you seek deeper understanding, wish to bring light to hidden aspects of a situation, or need guidance that cuts through confusion. By invoking the energy of the firefly, you tap into the power of seeing through the dark and bringing clarity to even the most obscure issues.

The Symbolism of Fireflies in Magic

Fireflies, or lightning bugs, are often seen as symbols of illumination, guidance, and the power of a small light in the vast darkness. In magical practices, fireflies are used to represent the uncovering of hidden knowledge, the spark of inspiration, and the ephemeral yet profound moments of insight. This spell channels the firefly's light to shine into the hidden corners of your life, helping you reveal the truths you seek and see with newfound clarity.

Ideal Timing and Preparations

- **Best Time for the Ritual:** Perform this spell during a new moon (for uncovering hidden aspects) or on a clear night when the stars are visible, emphasizing the theme of illumination in darkness.

- **Location:** Outdoors at night, preferably in a garden or natural space where fireflies might be present, or indoors near an open window or lit by candles.
- **Mindset:** Approach the ritual with an inquisitive spirit and an open mind. Be prepared to receive whatever truths come to light, even if they may challenge your current understanding.

Materials Needed

- A small lantern or a jar with holes (representing the firefly's light)
- A black or dark blue candle (symbolizing the night and mystery)
- A yellow or white candle (representing the firefly's light and truth)
- A piece of clear quartz or citrine (for clarity and illumination)
- Dried chamomile or bay leaves (to enhance truth-seeking)
- A small mirror (for reflection and insight)
- A piece of paper and a pen
- Essential oil such as lemon or frankincense (optional, for mental clarity)

The Ritual: Step-by-Step Guide

1. **Set Up Your Sacred Space** Choose a quiet outdoor space or a room with a window that opens to the night sky. Place the black or dark blue candle and the yellow or white candle side by side, representing darkness and light. Arrange the clear quartz or citrine, dried herbs, and small mirror around the candles. Position the lantern or jar in front of the candles.
2. **Cleanse the Space** Before starting, close your eyes and take a few deep breaths. Visualize a gentle breeze clearing away stagnant energy and creating a clean, welcoming space for your ritual. Say:
"*Night of stars, dark and still,
Cleanse this space, bend to my will.*

*Make it pure, make it right,
Ready now for truth and light."*

3. **Light the Dark Candle** Light the black or dark blue candle and say: *"Candle of night, deep and wide,
Show me shadows, where truths hide.
Darkness holds what I seek,
Hidden answers, silent and meek."*

Let the flame of the dark candle represent the unknown or hidden aspects of your situation.

1. **Add the Herbs to the Lantern** Place the dried chamomile or bay leaves into the lantern or jar, symbolizing the infusion of truth and clarity. If you are using essential oil, add a drop to the herbs. Say: *"Herbs of light, herbs of truth,
Guide me now, reveal my youth.
Wisdom old, insight bright,
Bring forth knowledge in the night."*
2. **Light the Light Candle** Light the yellow or white candle and focus on its glow. Say: *"Candle of light, flame so bright,
Reveal the truth, banish the night.
By firefly's glow, soft and fair,
Bring me insight, clear and rare."*

This candle represents the illumination that will pierce through the darkness, just as a firefly's light does.

1. **Hold the Crystal** Take the clear quartz or citrine in your hand, feeling its smooth surface and cool energy. Imagine it absorbing the dual energy of light and dark from the candles. Say: *"Crystal clear, shining bright,
Hold the power of this night.*

*Show me truth, sharp and bold,
Reveal the secrets untold."*

2. **Set Your Intention** On the piece of paper, write down what hidden truth or clarity you seek. Be specific, such as *"What is the true nature of [situation]?"* or *"Reveal what I need to know about [relationship]."* Place the paper inside the lantern or jar.
3. **Reflect with the Mirror** Hold the small mirror up to your face, allowing the candlelight to reflect onto it. Gaze into the mirror and imagine it showing the truths hidden within you or around you. Say: *"Mirror bright, mirror true,
Reflect the wisdom, bring it through.
What's concealed, now reveal,
Show me truth, make it real."*
4. **Final Visualization** Close your eyes and visualize a soft light, like that of a firefly, appearing in the dark. See this light moving through your mind, revealing hidden corners and bringing clarity wherever it goes. Hold this visualization for several minutes, allowing any thoughts, images, or insights to come to you naturally.
5. **Conclude the Ritual** Open your eyes and extinguish the black or dark blue candle, saying: *"Thank you, night, for what you hold,
Secrets whispered, truths retold.
Darkness fades, light shall stay,
Guiding me in a brighter way."*

Leave the yellow or white candle to burn for a few more minutes before extinguishing it. Remove the paper from the lantern or jar and, if possible, keep it under your pillow or in a journal to revisit your insights the next morning.

Post-Ritual Practices

- **Keep the Crystal Nearby:** Carry the clear quartz or citrine with you to maintain the clarity and insight gained from the ritual.

- **Review Your Insights:** Reflect on any thoughts or feelings that arose during the ritual. Write them in a journal to solidify your understanding.
- **Dream Recall:** If you keep the paper under your pillow, pay attention to your dreams that night. They may offer additional truths or symbols related to your inquiry.

Enhancements for More Potency

- **Use Firefly-Inspired Music:** Play soft, ethereal music or recordings of nighttime nature sounds to create an ambiance that enhances the ritual.
- **Add a Truth-Chant:** Repeat a chant such as *"Let the light reveal the unseen"* during your visualization.
- **Infuse Water with Moonlight:** Leave a bowl of water under the moon to absorb its light and sip a small amount after the ritual to internalize the energy of illumination.

Practical Applications of the Spell

The *Firefly's Light of Truth* spell is particularly useful when you need clarity on matters involving relationships, personal decisions, or hidden motives. It can be performed during times of doubt or confusion when you seek understanding that cuts through misinformation or emotional fog. The ritual's symbolism and elements work together to illuminate the unseen, helping you approach situations with a clearer perspective.

Embrace the quiet glow of the firefly and let it light your path, guiding you through the darkness to the answers you seek. This spell invites you to trust in the small, persistent light within, capable of uncovering even the deepest truths and leading you toward wisdom and understanding.

Chapter 23: The Berry Blessing of Health

A spell to promote vitality and long-lasting health

Introduction to the Spell

For centuries, berries have been revered for their health-boosting properties and powerful symbolism in various cultures. Rich in vitamins, antioxidants, and vibrant energy, berries symbolize vitality, protection, and life force. The *Berry Blessing of Health* spell is designed to harness the nourishing power of berries to promote overall health and long-lasting wellness. This ritual incorporates the natural energy of berries, combined with earth and healing symbolism, to create a spell that infuses the body with renewed strength and resilience.

Ideal for moments when you wish to fortify your health, regain energy, or set intentions for continuous well-being, this spell uses the vibrant life force of berries to imbue your spirit and body with vitality. It's perfect as part of a wellness practice or whenever you feel the need for a health boost.

The Symbolism of Berries in Magic

Berries are associated with growth, nourishment, and protection due to their vibrant colors and rich nutrients. In folklore and magic, berries represent vitality, regeneration, and the sweetness of life. Each type of berry carries unique properties, such as blackberries for protection and strength, blueberries for clarity and health, and raspberries for love and vitality. This spell taps into the essence of these fruits to create a ritual that promotes holistic health and well-being.

Ideal Timing and Preparations

- **Best Time for the Ritual:** This spell is best performed during the waxing moon (to build energy and health) or on a Sunday, which is associated with vitality and life force. Early morning, as the day begins, symbolizes new energy and renewal.
- **Location:** Outdoors in a garden or indoor space surrounded by plants or natural elements.

- **Mindset:** Approach the ritual with gratitude for the health you have and a genuine desire for growth in well-being. Be open to the energy of renewal and nurturing.

Materials Needed

- A red or green candle (representing life and vitality)
- A small bowl of mixed fresh or dried berries (such as blueberries, blackberries, and raspberries)
- Fresh mint leaves or thyme (for added health benefits and clarity)
- A piece of carnelian or green aventurine (stones associated with health and vitality)
- A small bowl of spring water (to represent life and nourishment)
- A piece of paper and a pen
- Essential oil such as lemon or eucalyptus (optional, for invigoration)
- A clean cloth or scarf (optional, for symbolic wrapping and protection)

The Ritual: Step-by-Step Guide

1. **Set Up Your Sacred Space** Choose a space that is serene and connected to nature. Place the red or green candle in the center and surround it with the bowl of berries, the mint leaves or thyme, the crystal, and the bowl of spring water. If using essential oil, anoint the candle with a drop to infuse it with invigorating energy.
2. **Cleanse the Space** Before beginning, close your eyes and visualize a warm, golden light filling your space and purifying it. Take a few deep breaths and say: *"Golden light, pure and bright,*
Cleanse this space, renew my sight.
Bring health, bring strength, bring life,
Protect this space from harm and strife."

3. **Ground and Center** Sit comfortably with your feet planted on the ground. Close your eyes, breathe deeply, and imagine roots growing from your body into the earth, connecting you to its nurturing energy. Feel grounded and at peace, ready to receive the vitality you are seeking.
4. **Light the Candle** Light the red or green candle and let its flame symbolize life force and renewal. Say: *"Candle of health, candle of might,*
Ignite my spirit, burn so bright.
Fill me with vigor, strength, and cheer,
Protect my body, year by year."
5. **Hold the Berries** Take the bowl of berries in your hands, feeling their coolness and vibrant energy. Visualize the nutrients and life force they hold. Say: *"Berries of red, black, and blue,*
Infuse me with health, strong and true.
Sweet and rich, nature's gift,
Bring vitality, let my spirit lift."
6. **Add the Herbs** Sprinkle fresh mint leaves or thyme into the bowl of berries, imagining them amplifying the health-giving energy. Say: *"Herbs of life, herbs of green,*
Add your power, pure and clean.
Heal and protect, nourish and grow,
Let health and vigor flow."
7. **Empower with the Crystal** Hold the carnelian or green aventurine in your dominant hand, feeling its warmth and energy spread through your body. Visualize it merging with the energy of the berries and herbs. Say: *"Stone of health, stone of light,*
Strengthen my body, day and night.
Guide my cells, renew each part,
Bring lasting health to mind and heart."
8. **Set Your Intention** On the piece of paper, write a specific affirmation or intention related to health, such as *"I am strong,*

healthy, and full of life." Place the paper under the bowl of water, symbolizing nourishment and the flow of vitality.

9. **Create a Symbolic Gesture** Take the clean cloth or scarf and gently place it over the bowl of berries and herbs. This represents the act of protecting and nurturing your health. Say: *"Cloth of care, cover so tight,*
Shield my health, guard my light.
Wrapped in safety, growth shall come,
Health renewed, troubles undone."

10. **Drink and Bless the Water** Dip your fingers in the bowl of spring water and touch your forehead, temples, and heart. Visualize the water energizing and purifying your body. Say: *"Water pure, water bright,*
Flow within, bring health's delight.
Bless my body, keep it strong,
Let vitality in me belong."

If desired, take a sip of the water as a symbolic act of internalizing the ritual's power.

1. **Conclude the Ritual** Extinguish the candle with gratitude and say: *"Thank you, flame, thank you, earth,*
For this spell of strength and worth.
Berries bright, herbs so green,
Health and joy, let them be seen."

Keep the bowl of berries in a special place for the rest of the day as a reminder of the spell's energy. Dispose of the berries and herbs respectfully the next day, either by consuming them if fresh or returning them to nature.

Post-Ritual Practices

- **Carry the Crystal:** Keep the carnelian or green aventurine with you to maintain the energy of vitality throughout your day.
- **Eat Nourishing Foods:** Incorporate berries and fresh herbs into your meals to reinforce the spell's power and connect with the physical manifestation of health.
- **Repeat the Affirmation:** Say your written affirmation daily to keep the spell's intention alive.

Enhancements for More Potency

- **Infuse Herbal Tea:** Brew a tea with mint or thyme and sip it while repeating your health affirmation.
- **Add Uplifting Music:** Play calming or nature-inspired music to amplify the serene and revitalizing energy of the ritual.
- **Daily Sun Ritual:** Spend a few moments each day standing in sunlight, visualizing the rays infusing you with strength and energy.

Practical Applications of the Spell

The *Berry Blessing of Health* spell is especially beneficial when you are recovering from illness, need an energy boost, or wish to maintain long-term wellness. It can be performed regularly as part of your self-care routine or whenever you feel the need for extra physical and emotional support. The ritual helps remind you that health is a holistic balance of body, mind, and spirit, drawing on the nurturing powers of nature.

By harnessing the vibrant life energy of berries, herbs, and crystal power, you channel vitality into your life, creating a foundation of strength and well-being. Let this spell be a cornerstone in your practice for health and renewal, celebrating the rich, natural gifts of the earth that support you in living a full and healthy life.

Chapter 24: Whispering Pines Serenity Spell
A calming spell for peace and serenity using pine needles

Introduction to the Spell

Pine trees, with their steadfast presence and soothing whispers in the wind, have long been symbols of peace, resilience, and tranquility. Their fresh, earthy scent and evergreen nature evoke a sense of calm and stability, even in the face of adversity. The *Whispering Pines Serenity Spell* is designed to channel the calming energy of pine needles to promote peace, reduce stress, and create an environment of serenity. This spell harnesses the natural qualities of pine to center your mind, calm your spirit, and foster a sense of profound inner peace.

Ideal for moments when life feels chaotic or overwhelming, this spell can be used as part of a regular relaxation ritual or whenever you need to create a serene space for meditation, rest, or contemplation. By connecting with the grounded energy of pine, you can draw on its timeless wisdom and tranquility to bring balance and harmony into your life.

The Symbolism of Pine in Magic

Pine trees are associated with endurance, longevity, and resilience due to their ability to remain green throughout the year. In many traditions, pine needles are used for purification, protection, and healing. Their scent and presence are believed to dispel negative energy and promote clarity of mind. The rustling sound of wind through pine branches is said to carry messages of peace and wisdom, connecting us to the natural world and reminding us of the calm that lies within.

Ideal Timing and Preparations

- **Best Time for the Ritual:** This spell is best performed during the waning moon (to release stress and promote relaxation) or on a Monday, a day associated with emotional balance and calm. Early evening is ideal for creating a peaceful transition into the night.
- **Location:** Outdoors beneath a pine tree or indoors with fresh or dried pine needles and a view of nature, if possible.

- **Mindset:** Approach this ritual with a sense of openness and readiness to let go of tension. Embrace the idea of surrendering to the calm and peace that nature provides.

Materials Needed

- A green or white candle (representing peace and tranquility)
- A small bowl of fresh or dried pine needles
- A piece of clear quartz or amethyst (for enhancing relaxation and mental clarity)
- A small sachet or piece of cloth (for creating a pine charm)
- A bowl of saltwater (for purification)
- Essential oil such as pine or cedarwood (optional, for deeper connection)
- A comfortable chair or meditation cushion

The Ritual: Step-by-Step Guide

1. **Set Up Your Sacred Space** Choose a space where you feel at ease. Place the green or white candle at the center, surrounded by the bowl of pine needles, clear quartz or amethyst, and the bowl of saltwater. Arrange the sachet or cloth nearby. If using essential oil, anoint the candle with a drop to enhance its calming properties.
2. **Cleanse the Space** Before starting, dip your fingers into the bowl of saltwater and sprinkle a few drops around your space to purify it. Visualize the saltwater absorbing any stress or negative energy. Say: *"Water of earth, pure and bright,*
Cleanse this space, bring tranquil light.
Let all tension, let all strain,
Wash away like falling rain."
3. **Ground and Center** Sit comfortably with your feet planted firmly on the ground. Close your eyes and take deep, slow breaths. Imagine roots extending from your body deep into the

earth, grounding you and connecting you to the steady, calming energy of the pine tree. Feel yourself becoming calm and centered.

4. **Light the Candle** Light the green or white candle and say: *"Candle of peace, candle of light,*
Bring serenity to this night.
Glow so gentle, flame so warm,
Keep me safe from any storm."

5. **Hold the Pine Needles** Take the bowl of pine needles in your hands and close your eyes. Inhale their scent and feel their earthy energy infusing you with calm. Visualize yourself standing in a forest, surrounded by tall pine trees, their soft whispers calming your mind. Say: *"Pines that whisper, pines so tall,*
Grant me peace, heed my call.
Let your essence, pure and fine,
Calm my spirit, still my mind."

6. **Empower with the Crystal** Hold the clear quartz or amethyst in your dominant hand and feel its cool, soothing energy. Imagine it amplifying the peace you draw from the pine. Say: *"Crystal clear, amethyst bright,*
Hold my calm, enhance my light.
Banish worry, soothe my soul,
Make my mind serene and whole."

7. **Create the Pine Charm** Place a handful of the pine needles into the sachet or cloth and tie it closed. This charm will serve as a reminder of the peace and serenity you are invoking. Hold it close to your heart and say: *"Charm of pine, nature's balm,*
Carry with you this perfect calm.
Wherever I go, day or night,
Keep my spirit safe and light."

8. **Anoint Yourself** Dip your fingers into the bowl of saltwater and touch your forehead, temples, and heart. Visualize the water absorbing any remaining tension and leaving behind a sense of tranquility. Say: *"Water pure, touch so light,*

Bring me peace, set things right.
Let the calm within me grow,
Like the pines, steady and slow."

9. **Reflect in Stillness** Sit quietly with the candle's glow and the scent of the pine needles surrounding you. Close your eyes and listen for any internal whispers or feelings that arise, just as you would listen to the wind moving through the pine branches. Let yourself be fully present in the moment for at least 10-15 minutes.

10. **Conclude the Ritual** To close the ritual, thank the energies of the pine, the earth, and your sacred space. Extinguish the candle and say: *"Thank you, pines, for peace so true,*
For bringing calm where it was due.
With gratitude, I end this spell,
In perfect peace, all is well."

Place the pine charm near your bed or workspace as a token of the ritual's energy and a reminder of the serenity you've cultivated.

Post-Ritual Practices

- **Keep the Pine Charm Nearby:** Carry the sachet with you or place it in an area where you spend a lot of time to maintain the spell's calming energy.
- **Practice Daily Breaths:** Take moments throughout your day to close your eyes and visualize the peaceful pine forest, reinforcing the sense of calm.
- **Use the Crystal for Meditation:** Meditate with the clear quartz or amethyst regularly to enhance and maintain your inner peace.

Enhancements for More Potency

- **Add Nature Sounds:** Play soft sounds of the forest or wind in the pines during the ritual to deepen your connection to nature.

- **Repeat a Mantra:** Use a calming mantra such as *"I am calm, I am peaceful"* during moments of stress to tap into the spell's energy.
- **Use Pine Incense:** Burn pine incense to invoke the energy of the pine tree and maintain a serene atmosphere.

Practical Applications of the Spell

The *Whispering Pines Serenity Spell* is perfect for times of high stress, before important events, or when you need to create a space of peace and relaxation. It can be used as part of a daily practice for stress management or as a way to unwind after a busy day. The calming energy of pine combined with the symbolic ritual elements encourages a state of lasting tranquility, promoting a sense of safety and well-being.

By incorporating the essence of pine, you align yourself with its timeless and unyielding peace. Let this spell be a refuge in your life, reminding you that, like the pine tree, you can stand tall and serene, regardless of the chaos that surrounds you. Embrace the whispering pines and let them guide you to a state of calm, balance, and serenity.

Chapter 25: The Willow's Compassion Ritual
A spell for fostering empathy, compassion, and emotional balance

Introduction to the Spell

The willow tree is a symbol of flexibility, resilience, and gentle strength. Known for its graceful, sweeping branches and its ability to thrive near water, the willow represents the balance between yielding to emotion and standing strong through adversity. The *Willow's Compassion Ritual* is designed to channel the nurturing energy of the willow to foster empathy, compassion, and emotional balance. This ritual helps you connect deeply with your own emotions and those of others, promoting understanding and kindness in relationships and within yourself.

This spell is ideal when you need to cultivate compassion, strengthen emotional bonds, or find emotional balance in challenging situations. By drawing on the soothing energy of the willow, you can create a space of openness, healing, and deeper emotional awareness.

The Symbolism of the Willow in Magic

The willow tree, often associated with water, is revered for its connection to intuition, emotion, and healing. In magical traditions, the willow is a tree of lunar energy, tied to the cycles of the moon and the ebb and flow of emotions. It embodies the idea that true strength comes from the ability to bend without breaking. This ritual utilizes the willow's attributes to help you embrace compassion, understand your emotions, and foster empathy toward others.

Ideal Timing and Preparations

- **Best Time for the Ritual:** This ritual is most effective during a full moon (to amplify emotional awareness) or a waning moon (to balance emotions). Dusk, when the day transitions to night, symbolizes introspection and the softening of energy.
- **Location:** Outdoors near a willow tree or a body of water if possible, or indoors with willow branches or pictures of willows for symbolism.
- **Mindset:** Approach this ritual with an open heart and a willingness to connect with your emotions and those of others. Prepare to release judgments and embrace understanding.

Materials Needed

- A silver or blue candle (representing empathy, emotion, and balance)
- A small bowl of water (to connect with the willow's association with water and emotion)
- Fresh or dried willow branches or leaves (for symbolic connection)
- A piece of rose quartz or moonstone (stones of compassion and emotional healing)
- A small piece of paper and a pen
- Essential oil such as lavender or chamomile (optional, for calm and balance)
- A soft cloth or scarf (optional, for comfort and reflection)

The Ritual: Step-by-Step Guide

1. **Set Up Your Sacred Space** Choose a serene space, ideally near a willow tree or a water source. Place the silver or blue candle at the center, surrounded by the bowl of water, willow branches, and crystal. Keep the piece of paper, pen, and soft cloth nearby. If using essential oil, anoint the candle with a drop for added calm.
2. **Cleanse the Space** Begin by sprinkling a few drops of water around your space to cleanse it, visualizing emotional balance and peace settling over the area. Say: *"Water pure, water bright,*
Cleanse this space, bring compassion's light.
Let all burdens and all strife,
Fade away, bring warmth to life."
3. **Ground and Center** Sit comfortably and close your eyes. Take deep, slow breaths and visualize roots extending from your body into the earth, grounding you. Imagine these roots connecting you to the ancient, nurturing energy of a willow tree, swaying gently with the wind. Feel yourself becoming balanced and calm.
4. **Light the Candle** Light the silver or blue candle and focus on its soft glow. Say: *"Candle of empathy, candle of peace,*
Bring forth compassion, let strife cease.
Flame so gentle, flame so wise,
Open my heart, open my eyes."
5. **Hold the Willow Branches** Take the willow branches or leaves in your hands and close your eyes. Feel their texture and let their symbolic energy wash over you, reminding you of the power of being flexible yet strong. Say: *"Willow's grace, willow's might,*
Guide my heart, hold it light.
Teach me wisdom, teach me care,
Foster love that I can share."
6. **Empower with the Crystal** Hold the rose quartz or moonstone in your dominant hand and imagine its warm, nurturing energy

spreading through you. Picture it expanding from your heart center and enveloping your whole body in a gentle, pink or white glow. Say: *"Crystal of love, crystal of grace,*
Bring compassion to this place.
Let understanding take its hold,
Make my heart tender, strong, and bold."

7. **Set Your Intention** On the piece of paper, write down an intention related to empathy or emotional balance, such as *"I embrace compassion and understanding toward myself and others."* Fold the paper and place it under the bowl of water, symbolizing the nurturing properties of water and the emotional support of the willow.

8. **Connect with the Water** Dip your fingers in the bowl of water and touch your forehead, temples, and heart. Visualize the water calming your mind and nurturing your emotions, bringing you into a state of balance. Say: *"Water so calm, water so deep,*
Help me listen, help me keep
The heart's wisdom, pure and true,
Foster compassion in all I do."

9. **Wrap Yourself for Reflection** Take the soft cloth or scarf and wrap it gently around your shoulders or hold it in your lap as a symbol of comfort and self-compassion. Close your eyes and imagine yourself sitting under the branches of a willow tree, surrounded by peace and understanding. Spend at least 10-15 minutes in this state of reflection, listening to any feelings or insights that arise.

10. **Conclude the Ritual** To close the ritual, thank the willow and the energies you have invoked. Extinguish the candle with gratitude and say: *"Thank you, willow, for your grace,*
For bringing peace to this space.
Compassion here, balance found,
With open heart, I am unbound."

Place the crystal on your bedside table or in a space where you often reflect or meditate as a reminder of the compassion you have cultivated.

Post-Ritual Practices

- **Keep the Crystal Close:** Carry the rose quartz or moonstone with you to maintain the energy of compassion and balance throughout your day.
- **Practice Mindful Listening:** Make an effort to listen deeply when communicating with others, embodying the empathy invoked during the ritual.
- **Repeat Daily Affirmations:** Recite your written intention or create a simple affirmation like *"I am compassionate and understanding"* to reinforce the spell's effects.

Enhancements for More Potency

- **Use Gentle Music:** Play soft, soothing music or nature sounds to create a calming atmosphere during the ritual.
- **Meditate with Willow Imagery:** Visualize yourself walking through a grove of willow trees, feeling their peaceful energy enveloping you.
- **Incorporate Moonlight:** Perform the ritual outdoors during a full moon or place the bowl of water under moonlight for an hour before the ritual to amplify its effects.

Practical Applications of the Spell

The *Willow's Compassion Ritual* is perfect for fostering emotional balance during difficult conversations, deepening empathy in relationships, or simply nurturing a compassionate mindset. It can be performed regularly to cultivate emotional resilience and understanding or used in moments when you need to reconnect with your inner sense of calm and compassion.

By drawing on the willow's gentle yet strong energy, you learn to be flexible in your approach to emotions and relationships. This ritual helps you find strength in empathy and balance in understanding, allowing you to build deeper connections with others and within yourself. Embrace the wisdom of the willow and let it guide you to a life filled with compassion, empathy, and emotional harmony.

Appendices
Appendix A: Guide to Spell Materials

An in-depth guide to understanding the significance and use of spell materials

In any spell or ritual, the choice of materials plays a crucial role in amplifying the energy and intentions set by the practitioner. Each item carries its own vibrational frequency, symbolism, and history of magical use. This guide will provide comprehensive insight into the common spell materials used throughout *The Evergreen Spellbook*, explaining their meanings, properties, and best practices for use.

1. Candles

Symbolism and Use: Candles are one of the most versatile tools in magic. The flame represents the element of fire, symbolizing transformation, energy, and illumination. The color of the candle enhances the specific intention of the spell.

Color Meanings:

- **White:** Purity, protection, and peace. Used for cleansing and general purposes.
- **Green:** Growth, prosperity, and healing. Ideal for spells involving health or financial abundance.
- **Blue:** Tranquility, emotional healing, and communication. Used for peace and deep emotional work.
- **Red:** Passion, strength, and vitality. Often used for spells involving energy and courage.

- **Black:** Protection, banishing negative energy, and transformation. Effective for removing obstacles.
- **Yellow:** Creativity, confidence, and intellect. Used for inspiration and boosting mental clarity.

Best Practices: Always anoint candles with an essential oil that corresponds to your intention to deepen their energy. Light the candle with focused intent, visualizing the flame embodying your goal.

2. Crystals and Stones

Symbolism and Use: Crystals are natural energy conductors that amplify and direct intention. Each stone has unique properties that make it suited to particular types of magic.

Common Crystals:

- **Clear Quartz:** Amplification, clarity, and healing. Known as the "master healer," it enhances any spell's energy.
- **Amethyst:** Intuition, peace, and spiritual growth. Great for emotional balance and insight.
- **Rose Quartz:** Love, compassion, and emotional healing. Used for spells related to relationships and self-love.
- **Citrine:** Abundance, joy, and prosperity. Ideal for financial growth and boosting positivity.
- **Carnelian:** Creativity, courage, and motivation. Used to break creative blocks and enhance confidence.
- **Green Aventurine:** Luck, health, and growth. Suited for healing and prosperity spells.
- **Moonstone:** Intuition, feminine energy, and emotional harmony. Effective for spells involving emotions and the moon's energy.

Best Practices: Cleanse your crystals before use by placing them in moonlight, using sage smoke, or immersing them in a bowl of saltwater (ensure the crystal type is water-safe). Hold your crystal while setting your intention and visualize its energy enhancing your spell.

3. Herbs and Plants

Symbolism and Use: Herbs and plants have been used in magic for centuries, carrying the wisdom of nature and the properties of their environment.

Common Herbs and Their Meanings:

- **Sage:** Purification, protection, and wisdom. Used to cleanse spaces and prepare for rituals.
- **Lavender:** Peace, healing, and tranquility. Perfect for spells involving relaxation and emotional healing.
- **Rosemary:** Protection, memory, and clarity. Often used in purification rituals.
- **Mint:** Clarity, prosperity, and mental stimulation. Enhances focus and energy.
- **Thyme:** Courage, healing, and purification. Used for health-related spells.
- **Chamomile:** Calm, luck, and prosperity. Ideal for spells involving relaxation and attracting positive energy.
- **Pine Needles:** Resilience, protection, and peace. Used for grounding and calming spells.

Best Practices: Fresh herbs are generally more potent, but dried herbs are more convenient and longer-lasting. Crush or burn herbs as part of your ritual, or steep them into teas for spells that require internal work.

4. Essential Oils

Symbolism and Use: Essential oils concentrate the energy of plants and flowers, allowing for targeted enhancements of your rituals.

Popular Essential Oils and Their Properties:

- **Lavender Oil:** Calming and protective. Used for relaxation and emotional spells.
- **Frankincense Oil:** Spiritual connection, protection, and focus. Enhances meditation and deep introspection.
- **Lemon Oil:** Cleansing, clarity, and positivity. Used to uplift energy and refresh the mind.
- **Peppermint Oil:** Mental clarity, energy, and healing. Often used for spells involving focus and vitality.
- **Patchouli Oil:** Prosperity, grounding, and attraction. Ideal for spells involving abundance and stability.
- **Cedarwood Oil:** Strength, protection, and grounding. Enhances connection to the earth.

Best Practices: Always dilute essential oils with a carrier oil if applying to the skin. Anoint candles, crystals, or yourself to imbue your ritual with the essence of the oil's properties.

5. Candles, Incense, and Smoke

Symbolism and Use: Incense and smoke are associated with the element of air, representing thoughts, communication, and the carrying of intentions to the spiritual realm.

Common Incense Types:

- **Sandalwood:** Purity, protection, and spiritual awareness.
- **Frankincense:** Clarity, meditation, and connection to the divine.
- **Myrrh:** Healing, protection, and grounding.
- **Cinnamon:** Prosperity, passion, and increased energy.
- **Rose:** Love, attraction, and harmony.

Best Practices: Use incense to prepare the space by wafting smoke around the room or area. Light incense during the ritual to maintain a connection to the element of air.

6. Water

Symbolism and Use: Water is associated with intuition, healing, and emotional depth. It is an essential element in rituals involving cleansing, emotional work, and spiritual connection.

Types of Water for Rituals:

- **Spring Water:** Purity and life energy. Best for general purposes.
- **Moon-Charged Water:** Energy and intuition. Leave water under the full moon overnight for added lunar energy.
- **Saltwater:** Purification and protection. Used to cleanse tools and spaces.

Best Practices: Incorporate water in bowls or sprinkle it in your space to purify and invite emotional clarity. Sip moon-charged water after a ritual to internalize its energy.

7. Symbols and Natural Elements

Symbolism and Use: Symbols such as runes, sigils, and other markings enhance the intention of a spell. Natural elements, including stones, branches, and leaves, carry the wisdom and energy of the earth.

Common Symbols and Their Meanings:

- **Pentacle:** Protection, balance, and connection to the elements.
- **Spirals:** Growth, evolution, and cycles.
- **Ankh:** Life, immortality, and spiritual protection.

Best Practices: Draw symbols or carve them into candles to amplify the intention of the spell. Use natural elements from your environment, such as pine cones or branches, to ground your ritual and connect with nature's energy.

8. Charms and Sachets

Symbolism and Use: Charms and sachets are portable carriers of energy that keep the spell's power close to you. They can be made with herbs, crystals, and personal items to maintain the intention long after the ritual is complete.

Best Practices: Use cloth or pouches in colors that match your spell's goal. Fill them with dried herbs, small crystals, and a piece of paper with your intention written on it. Carry or place the charm in your home or workspace to keep the spell's energy active.

Conclusion

Choosing the right materials for your ritual is essential for harnessing the most potent energy for your spellwork. The materials you use should resonate with your personal energy and intentions, creating a seamless blend between your goals and nature's inherent power. Understanding the symbolism, properties, and applications of these elements allows you to craft rituals that are both effective and deeply meaningful.

Appendix B: Moon Phases and Their Impact on Spells

An extensive guide to understanding how the moon's phases influence spellwork

The moon has captivated humanity for millennia with its luminous glow and mysterious phases. In the realm of magic, the moon is revered for its profound influence on energy and spells. Each phase of the moon carries unique characteristics that align with different types of spellwork. By timing rituals to the moon's phases, practitioners can amplify their intentions and harness the natural energy cycles for greater effectiveness. This appendix provides an in-depth guide to the moon phases and how they impact various types of spells.

1. New Moon

Characteristics and Energy: The new moon is a time of new beginnings, potential, and planting seeds for the future. It marks the start of the lunar cycle when the moon is not visible in the sky. This phase symbolizes a clean slate and the quiet, fertile energy of creation.

Best for Spells Related To:

- Setting new intentions and goals
- Initiating new projects or relationships
- Manifesting personal growth and transformation
- Cleansing and banishing old habits or negativity

Common Rituals and Practices:

- **Setting Intentions:** Write down clear goals or desires that you want to manifest over the next moon cycle.
- **New Moon Water:** Leave a bowl of water outside under the new moon to create water infused with the energy of fresh starts.

- **Planting Seeds:** Literally or metaphorically plant seeds to symbolize new beginnings and the growth of your intentions.

Tips for New Moon Rituals: This is a great time for journaling, meditation, and quiet introspection. Use white or silver candles to enhance the energy of purity and new beginnings.

2. Waxing Crescent Moon

Characteristics and Energy: The waxing crescent phase follows the new moon and represents the phase of building energy and intention. As the moon grows in light, so does the potential for manifestation. This is the phase for taking initial action toward your goals.

Best for Spells Related To:

- Building momentum and motivation
- Strengthening commitment to new projects or habits
- Drawing positive energy and support for your intentions

Common Rituals and Practices:

- **Affirmations and Visualizations:** Reaffirm your intentions daily through positive affirmations and visualizing success.
- **Energy Charging:** Charge crystals and tools with your intentions to support continued progress.
- **Physical Action:** Begin taking tangible steps toward achieving your goals.

Tips for Waxing Crescent Rituals: Use herbs like rosemary and mint for energy and focus, and light green or yellow candles to encourage growth and inspiration.

3. First Quarter Moon

Characteristics and Energy: The first quarter moon is a period of action, growth, and decision-making. Half of the moon is illuminated, symbolizing balance and the need to confront challenges or obstacles that arise. This is a time for pushing forward with strength and determination.

Best for Spells Related To:

- Overcoming obstacles and challenges
- Gaining courage and strength
- Making decisions and taking definitive actions

Common Rituals and Practices:

- **Obstacle-Breaking Rituals:** Use this phase to perform spells that clear paths and remove blockages.
- **Courage Boosting:** Empower yourself with spells that boost confidence and assertiveness.
- **Commitment Rituals:** Revisit your intentions and reinforce your commitment to your goals.

Tips for First Quarter Rituals: Work with stones like carnelian and tiger's eye for strength and courage. Burn incense such as cinnamon or ginger to boost energy and determination.

4. Waxing Gibbous Moon

Characteristics and Energy: The waxing gibbous phase is a time of refinement and preparation. The moon is nearly full, and its energy is intense, signaling the culmination of efforts. This phase is ideal for reviewing progress and making any necessary adjustments to your plans.

Best for Spells Related To:

- Fine-tuning plans and intentions

- Attracting success and prosperity
- Preparing for major rituals or outcomes

Common Rituals and Practices:

- **Reflection and Adjustment:** Meditate on your progress and make any needed changes to your approach.
- **Prosperity Spells:** Cast spells to attract abundance and prosperity as the energy builds toward the full moon.
- **Gratitude Rituals:** Express gratitude for the progress made so far, fostering positive energy for completion.

Tips for Waxing Gibbous Rituals: Use crystals like citrine and green aventurine for prosperity and growth. Light gold or orange candles for motivation and success.

5. Full Moon

Characteristics and Energy: The full moon is the peak of the lunar cycle, a time of maximum energy and power. It is a period of illumination, completion, and celebration. The full moon's light reveals truths, magnifies intentions, and supports powerful manifestations.

Best for Spells Related To:

- Manifestation and culmination of goals
- Spiritual work and intuitive insight
- Healing and release
- Enhancing any type of spellwork

Common Rituals and Practices:

- **Manifestation Rituals:** Cast powerful spells to manifest desires set during the new moon.

- **Releasing Ceremonies:** Use the full moon's energy to release anything that no longer serves you, whether physical, emotional, or spiritual.
- **Charging and Cleansing:** Place crystals, tools, and talismans under the moonlight to cleanse and recharge them with lunar energy.

Tips for Full Moon Rituals: Use white, silver, or blue candles for spiritual work and reflection. Incorporate moonstone and selenite for deepening intuition and connection to lunar energy.

6. Waning Gibbous Moon (Disseminating Moon)

Characteristics and Energy: The waning gibbous phase begins as the full moon starts to diminish in light. It is a time of sharing knowledge, gratitude, and introspection. The focus shifts from manifestation to reflection and generosity.

Best for Spells Related To:

- Gratitude and giving thanks
- Sharing wisdom and knowledge
- Reflecting on lessons learned

Common Rituals and Practices:

- **Gratitude Practices:** Reflect on your achievements and express gratitude for the support received.
- **Spiritual Cleansing:** Use this time for gentle cleansing rituals that prepare you for the coming release.
- **Sharing and Teaching:** Share your knowledge and experiences with others, fostering community and support.

Tips for Waning Gibbous Rituals: Use herbs like chamomile and sage for gratitude and cleansing. Light white or pink candles for gentle reflection and peace.

7. Last Quarter Moon

Characteristics and Energy: The last quarter moon is a time for release, forgiveness, and letting go. As the moon continues to wane, this phase is perfect for removing what no longer serves you and breaking ties with past habits or relationships that hold you back.

Best for Spells Related To:

- Letting go of negative energy or attachments
- Forgiveness and emotional release
- Reflection and preparation for new beginnings

Common Rituals and Practices:

- **Release Rituals:** Write down what you need to release and safely burn the paper, symbolizing letting go.
- **Cleansing Baths:** Take a ritual bath infused with Epsom salts and lavender to cleanse your spirit.
- **Cord-Cutting Rituals:** Use a symbolic cord-cutting ceremony to release energetic ties to people or situations.

Tips for Last Quarter Rituals: Work with black tourmaline or obsidian for protection and release. Burn incense like myrrh or frankincense to clear the space of lingering energy.

8. Waning Crescent Moon (Balsamic Moon)

Characteristics and Energy: The waning crescent moon, also known as the balsamic moon, is the final phase of the lunar cycle. It is a time for rest, surrender, and recuperation before the new moon brings renewal. This phase invites introspection and quiet contemplation.

Best for Spells Related To:

- Rest, healing, and self-care
- Deep spiritual reflection and meditation
- Preparation for new intentions and goals

Common Rituals and Practices:

- **Meditation and Introspection:** Engage in meditation to reflect on the past lunar cycle and what it taught you.
- **Restorative Spells:** Cast spells that focus on healing and nurturing the body and spirit.
- **Journal Reflections:** Write down insights and lessons learned, preparing for the new cycle.

Tips for Waning Crescent Rituals: Use soft, soothing candles in colors like blue or lavender for calming energy. Incorporate amethyst or clear quartz for deep meditation and spiritual insight.

Conclusion

Understanding the moon's phases and aligning your spellwork with its energy can significantly enhance the effectiveness of your rituals. The moon's cycle reflects the natural ebb and flow of energy, providing opportunities to set intentions, take action, reflect, and release. By tapping into the unique qualities of each phase, practitioners can work in harmony with nature's rhythms, creating more powerful and balanced magical experiences.

Appendix C: Common Nature-Based Symbols and Their Meanings

An extensive guide to understanding the meanings and uses of nature-based symbols in magic

Nature has always served as an abundant source of inspiration and power in magical practices. Symbols derived from plants, animals, and natural phenomena are imbued with unique energies and meanings, making them integral components of spellwork and rituals. Understanding these symbols allows practitioners to incorporate them thoughtfully into their practice, enhancing the efficacy of spells and fostering a deeper connection with the natural world. This appendix explores common nature-based symbols, their meanings, and practical applications in magical practice.

1. Tree Symbols

General Meaning: Trees represent life, growth, stability, and connection between the physical and spiritual realms. Each type of tree carries its own unique properties that can be harnessed in spells.

Notable Trees and Their Symbolism:

- **Oak Tree:** Strength, endurance, and protection. The oak is considered a sacred tree in many cultures, symbolizing power and resilience.
- **Willow Tree:** Flexibility, intuition, and healing. Known for its graceful branches, the willow represents emotional wisdom and the ability to adapt.
- **Pine Tree:** Protection, peace, and resilience. Pine trees symbolize longevity and steadfastness.
- **Ash Tree:** Transformation, connection, and spiritual knowledge. The ash is often associated with the concept of the world tree in mythology.

Applications in Spellwork: Use oak leaves or acorns for protection spells, willow branches in rituals for emotional balance, and pine needles for creating a peaceful atmosphere.

2. Plant and Flower Symbols

General Meaning: Plants and flowers embody the essence of nature's beauty and power, each bringing its own vibrational energy to rituals.

Key Plants and Flowers:

- **Lavender:** Peace, purification, and relaxation. Lavender is used in rituals to cleanse energy and promote calm.
- **Rose:** Love, passion, and healing. The rose is a powerful symbol of emotional depth and connection.
- **Mint:** Clarity, prosperity, and energy. Mint leaves are excellent for spells that require mental sharpness and focus.
- **Dandelion:** Wishes, resilience, and hope. The dandelion represents the ability to rise above challenges and is often used in spells for wish fulfillment.
- **Thyme:** Courage, protection, and purification. Used to boost confidence and protect against negative energy.

Applications in Spellwork: Place fresh or dried lavender in sachets for sleep and peace spells, incorporate rose petals in love rituals, and burn thyme to cleanse a space of negative energy.

3. Animal Symbols

General Meaning: Animals are revered for their qualities and characteristics, serving as guides or totems in magical practices.

Prominent Animal Symbols:

- **Butterfly:** Transformation, rebirth, and new beginnings. A powerful symbol for spells involving change and personal growth.
- **Owl:** Wisdom, intuition, and knowledge. Owls are often associated with uncovering hidden truths and deepening one's spiritual awareness.
- **Wolf:** Loyalty, intuition, and freedom. The wolf represents strong instincts and the power of community.
- **Deer:** Gentleness, compassion, and grace. Used in rituals that call for emotional balance and nurturing energy.
- **Raven:** Mystery, transformation, and protection. Ravens are seen as carriers of mystical knowledge and are used in spells for uncovering hidden information or guarding against negative forces.

Applications in Spellwork: Incorporate owl feathers or images in rituals to enhance intuition, use butterfly symbolism when casting spells for transformation, and call on the energy of the wolf for protective and instinctual spells.

4. Elemental Symbols

General Meaning: The elements of earth, air, fire, and water are foundational in magic, each symbolizing different aspects of life and spiritual practice.

Elemental Meanings:

- **Earth:** Stability, growth, and grounding. Associated with fertility, prosperity, and physical strength.
- **Air:** Communication, intellect, and inspiration. Air symbolizes thought, creativity, and the breath of life.
- **Fire:** Passion, transformation, and energy. It is a symbol of creation and destruction, used in spells for change and motivation.
- **Water:** Emotion, healing, and intuition. Water represents purification, reflection, and the subconscious mind.

Applications in Spellwork: Use stones and soil in grounding rituals for earth energy, burn incense or herbs for air, incorporate candle flames for fire spells, and add water to rituals for emotional cleansing and healing.

5. Celestial Symbols

General Meaning: Celestial bodies such as the sun, moon, and stars are powerful symbols representing cycles, time, and divine energy.

Celestial Bodies and Their Meanings:

- **Sun:** Vitality, strength, and power. The sun is used in spells for success, growth, and energizing life force.
- **Moon:** Intuition, cycles, and feminine energy. The moon's phases dictate the best timing for various types of spellwork.
- **Stars:** Guidance, hope, and destiny. Stars are associated with finding one's path and receiving guidance from higher realms.

- **Comets:** Sudden change, opportunity, and revelation. Comets are symbolic of significant and sometimes abrupt transformations.

Applications in Spellwork: Perform solar-based rituals at noon to harness the sun's peak energy for empowerment, conduct lunar rituals at different phases for intuitive and emotional work, and use star imagery to inspire hope and seek guidance.

6. Herb and Tree Parts
General Meaning: Specific parts of herbs and trees, such as roots, bark, and leaves, each carry distinct energies and meanings.

Key Parts and Their Symbolism:

- **Roots:** Stability, grounding, and ancestral wisdom. Roots are used in spells to connect with one's heritage or reinforce intentions.
- **Bark:** Protection, resilience, and support. Bark is often used for shielding spells and fortifying the energy of a space.
- **Leaves:** Growth, renewal, and adaptability. Leaves can symbolize fresh starts and are used in spells to foster growth.
- **Flowers:** Beauty, attraction, and manifestation. The blooms of plants add vibrancy and life to rituals.

Applications in Spellwork: Use roots in grounding rituals, burn bark for protective smoke, scatter leaves for growth spells, and incorporate flowers in attraction or love spells.

7. Natural Phenomena Symbols

General Meaning: Natural events and phenomena carry potent energy and can be called upon in magic for powerful effects.

Common Phenomena and Their Meanings:

- **Rain:** Cleansing, renewal, and emotional release. Rainwater is collected for purification rituals and spells to wash away negativity.
- **Thunderstorms:** Power, change, and intense energy. Used in spells that require a strong boost of force or to initiate transformation.
- **Sunrise:** New beginnings, hope, and potential. Ideal for rituals that set intentions or welcome a new chapter.
- **Fog:** Mystery, intuition, and the hidden. Fog is symbolic of deep introspection and accessing the subconscious mind.
- **Wind:** Change, communication, and freedom. The wind is invoked in spells for transitions and spreading messages or intentions.

Applications in Spellwork: Collect rainwater for purification rituals, conduct spells at sunrise to invite fresh starts, and incorporate wind chimes to harness the energy of the wind for communication.

8. Stone and Mineral Symbols

General Meaning: Stones and minerals represent the stability and ancient knowledge of the earth. They can be used in a variety of spells for grounding, protection, and energy amplification.

Common Stones and Their Meanings:

- **Obsidian:** Protection, grounding, and cutting ties. Ideal for defensive spells and clearing negative energy.
- **Jasper:** Nurturing, stability, and health. Used for spells related to well-being and emotional balance.
- **Hematite:** Grounding, strength, and mental clarity. Helps with focus and concentration.
- **Lapis Lazuli:** Wisdom, truth, and insight. Used in rituals for enhancing intuition and connecting with deeper truths.
- **Turquoise:** Healing, communication, and balance. Brings a sense of peace and spiritual attunement.

Applications in Spellwork: Carry obsidian for protection, place hematite on your workspace for mental focus, and use turquoise in spells for enhanced communication and healing.

Conclusion

Nature-based symbols carry deep, ancient meanings that enhance the energy and focus of magical work. By understanding and integrating these symbols into your practice, you can create more intentional and effective spells. These symbols help bridge the connection between the practitioner and the natural world, fostering a harmonious and powerful spellcasting experience. Use this guide to select and incorporate the symbols that best align with your intentions and resonate with your energy.

Message from the Author:

I hope you enjoyed this book, I love astrology and knew there was not a book such as this out on the shelf. I love metaphysical items as well. Please check out my other books:

-Life of Government Benefits

-My life of Hell

-My life with Hydrocephalus

-Red Sky

-World Domination:Woman's rule

-World Domination:Woman's Rule 2: The War

-Life and Banishment of Apophis: book 1

-The Kidney Friendly Diet

-The Ultimate Hemp Cookbook

-Creating a Dispensary(legally)

-Cleanliness throughout life: the importance of showering from childhood to adulthood.

-Strong Roots: The Risks of Overcoddling children

-Hemp Horoscopes: Cosmic Insights and Earthly Healing

- Celestial Hemp Navigating the Zodiac: Through the Green Cosmos

-Astrological Hemp: Aligning The Stars with Earth's Ancient Herb

-The Astrological Guide to Hemp: Stars, Signs, and Sacred Leaves

-Green Growth: Innovative Marketing Strategies for your Hemp Products and Dispensary

-Cosmic Cannabis

-Astrological Munchies

-Henry The Hemp

-Zodiacal Roots: The Astrological Soul Of Hemp

- **Green Constellations: Intersection of Hemp and Zodiac**

-Hemp in The Houses: An astrological Adventure Through The Cannabis Galaxy

-Galactic Ganja Guide

Heavenly Hemp
Zodiac Leaves
Doctor Who Astrology
Cannastrology
Stellar Satvias and Cosmic Indicas
<u>Celestial Cannabis: A Zodiac Journey</u>
AstroHerbology: The Sky and The Soil: Volume 1
AstroHerbology:Celestial Cannabis:Volume 2
Cosmic Cannabis Cultivation
The Starry Guide to Herbal Harmony: Volume 1
The Starry Guide to Herbal Harmony: Cannabis Universe: Volume 2

Yugioh Astrology: Astrological Guide to Deck, Duels and more
Nightmare Mansion: Echoes of The Abyss
Nightmare Mansion 2: Legacy of Shadows
Nightmare Mansion 3: Shadows of the Forgotten
Nightmare Mansion 4: Echoes of the Damned
The Life and Banishment of Apophis: Book 2
Nightmare Mansion: Halls of Despair
<u>Healing with Herb: Cannabis and Hydrocephalus</u>
Planetary Pot: Aligning with Astrological Herbs: Volume 1
Fast Track to Freedom: 30 Days to Financial Independence Using AI, Assets, and Agile Hustles
<u>Cosmic Hemp Pathways</u>
How to Become Financially Free in 30 Days: 10,000 Paths to Prosperity
Zodiacal Herbage: Astrological Insights: Volume 1
Nightmare Mansion: Whispers in the Walls
The Daleks Invade Atlantis
Henry the hemp and Hydrocephalus

10X The Kidney Friendly Diet
Cannabis Universe: Adult coloring book

Hemp Astrology: The Healing Power of the Stars
Zodiacal Herbage: Astrological Insights: Cannabis Universe: Volume 2
Planetary Pot: Aligning with Astrological Herbs: Cannabis Universes: Volume 2
Doctor Who Meets the Replicators and SG-1: The Ultimate Battle for Survival
Nightmare Mansion: Curse of the Blood Moon
The Celestial Stoner: A Guide to the Zodiac
Cosmic Pleasures: Sex Toy Astrology for Every Sign
Hydrocephalus Astrology: Navigating the Stars and Healing Waters
Lapis and the Mischievous Chocolate Bar

Celestial Positions: Sexual Astrology for Every Sign
Apophis's Shadow Work Journal: : A Journey of Self-Discovery and Healing
Kinky Cosmos: Sexual Kink Astrology for Every Sign
Digital Cosmos: The Astrological Digimon Compendium
Stellar Seeds: The Cosmic Guide to Growing with Astrology
Apophis's Daily Gratitude Journal

Cat Astrology: Feline Mysteries of the Cosmos
The Cosmic Kama Sutra: An Astrological Guide to Sexual Positions
Unleash Your Potential: A Guided Journal Powered by AI Insights
Whispers of the Enchanted Grove

Cosmic Pleasures: An Astrological Guide to Sexual Kinks
369, 12 Manifestation Journal
Whisper of the nocturne journal(blank journal for writing or drawing)

The Boogey Book
Locked In Reflection: A Chastity Journey Through Locktober
Generating Wealth Quickly:
How to Generate $100,000 in 24 Hours
Star Magic: Harness the Power of the Universe
The Flatulence Chronicles: A Fart Journal for Self-Discovery
The Doctor and The Death Moth
Seize the Day: A Personal Seizure Tracking Journal
The Ultimate Boogeyman Safari: A Journey into the Boogie World and Beyond
Whispers of Samhain: 1,000 Spells of Love, Luck, and Lunar Magic: Samhain Spell Book
Apophis's guides:
Witch's Spellbook Crafting Guide for Halloween
<u>**Frost & Flame: The Enchanted Yule Grimoire of 1000 Winter Spells**</u>
<u>**The Ultimate Boogey Goo Guide & Spooky Activities for Halloween Fun**</u>
Harmony of the Scales: A Libra's Spellcraft for Balance and Beauty
The Enchanted Advent: 36 Days of Christmas Wonders

Nightmare Mansion: The Labyrinth of Screams
Harvest of Enchantment: 1,000 Spells of Gratitude, Love, and Fortune for Thanksgiving
The Boogey Chronicles: A Journal of Nightly Encounters and Shadowy Secrets
The 12 Days of Financial Freedom: A Step-by-Step Christmas Countdown to Transform Your Finances
Sigil of the Eternal Spiral Blank Journal
A Christmas Feast: Timeless Recipes for Every Meal
Holiday Stress-Free Solutions: A Survival Guide to Thriving During the Festive Season

Yu-Gi-Oh! Holiday Gifting Mastery: The Ultimate Guide for Fans and Newcomers Alike

Holiday Harmony: A Hydrocephalus Survival Guide for the Festive Season

Celestial Craft: The Witch's Almanac for 2025 – A Cosmic Guide to Manifestations, Moons, and Mystical Events

Doctor Who: The Toymaker's Winter Wonderland

Tulsa King Unveiled: A Thrilling Guide to Stallone's Mafia Masterpiece

Pendulum Craft: A Complete Guide to Crafting and Using Personalized Divination Tools

Nightmare Mansion: Santa's Eternal Eve

Starlight Noel: A Cosmic Journey through Christmas Mysteries

The Dark Architect: Unlocking the Blueprint of Existence

Surviving the Embrace: The Ultimate Guide to Encounters with The Hugging Molly

The Enchanted Codex: Secrets of the Craft for Witches, Wiccans, and Pagans

Harvest of Gratitude: A Complete Thanksgiving Guide

Yuletide Essentials: A Complete Guide to an Authentic and Magical Christmas

Celestial Smokes: A Cosmic Guide to Cigars and Astrology

Living in Balance: A Comprehensive Survival Guide to Thriving with Diabetes Insipidus

Cosmic Symbiosis: The Venom Zodiac Chronicles

The Cursed Paw of Ambition

Cosmic Symbiosis: The Astrological Venom Journal

Celestial Wonders Unfold: A Stargazer's Guide to the Cosmos (2024-2029)

The Ultimate Black Friday Prepper's Guide: Mastering Shopping Strategies and Savings

Cosmic Sales: The Astrological Guide to Black Friday Shopping

Legends of the Corn Mother and Other Harvest Myths

Whispers of the Harvest: The Corn Mother's Journal

If you want solar for your home go here: https://www.harborsolar.live/apophisenterprises/

Get Some Tarot cards: https://www.makeplayingcards.com/sell/apophis-occult-shop

Get some shirts: https://www.bonfire.com/store/apophis-shirt-emporium/

Instagrams:
@apophis_enterprises,
@apophisbookemporium,
@apophisscardshop
Twitter: @apophisenterpr1
 Tiktok:@apophisenterprise
Youtube: @sg1fan23477, @FiresideRetreatKingdom
Hive: @sg1fan23477
CheeLee: @SG1fan23477

Podcast: Apophis Chat Zone: https://open.spotify.com/show/5zXbrCLEV2xzCp8ybrfHsk?si=fb4d4fdbdce44dec

Newsletter: https://apophiss-newsletter-27c897.beehiiv.com/